1970s

Ten Years of Popular Hits Arranged for EASY PIANO

Arranged by Dan Coates

DECADE by DECADE

ISBN-10: 0-7390-4721-3
ISBN-13: 978-0-7390-4721-7

Alfred

Contents

ANNIE'S SONG

"Annie's Song" was written by John Denver for his then-wife, Annie. It has become a wedding standard, and, interestingly, doesn't contain the word "Annie." It was Denver's second #1 song in the United States and his first and only hit single in the U.K.

Words and Music by John Denver
Arranged by Dan Coates

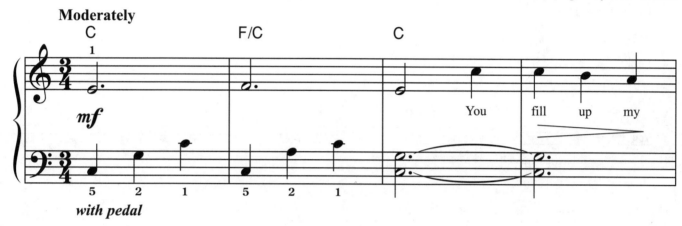

13 F · Em · Dm · F

spring - time, like a walk in the

17 G

rain. Like a storm in the

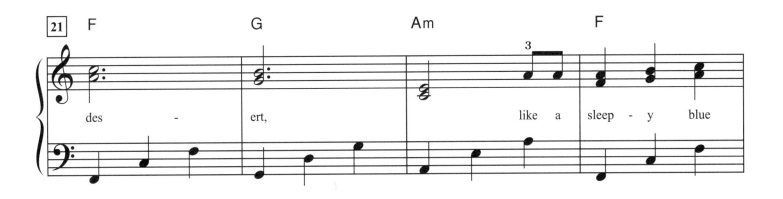

21 F · G · Am · F

des - ert, like a sleep - y blue

25 C · Em/B · Am · C/G

o - cean, you fill up my

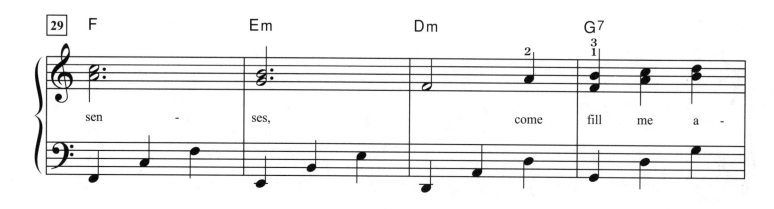

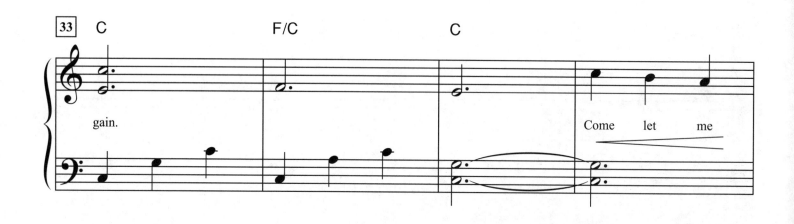

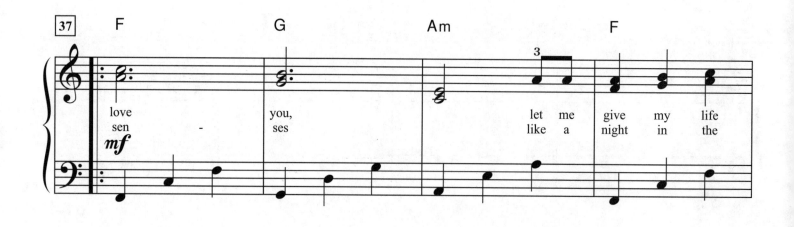

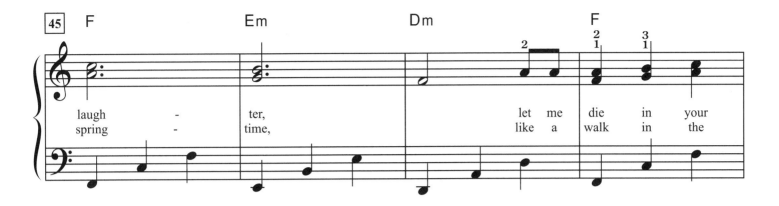

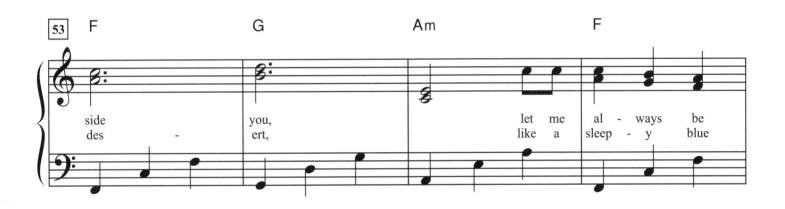

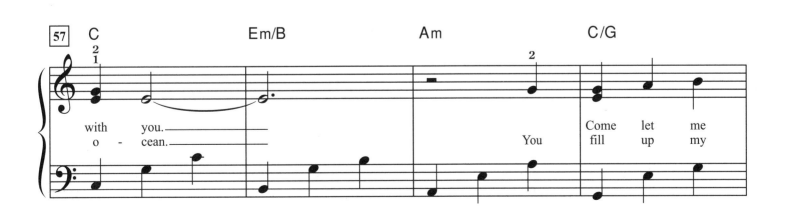

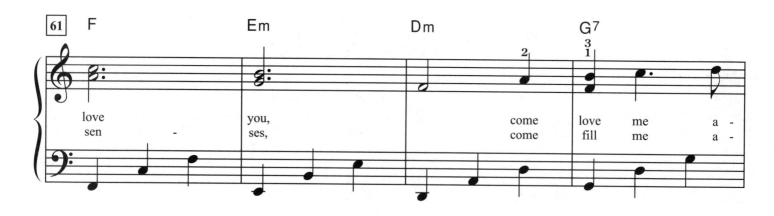

love
sen - ses,

come
come

love
fill

me
me

a -
a -

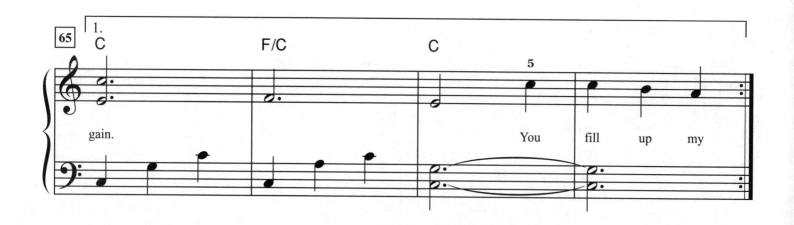

gain.

You fill up my

gain.

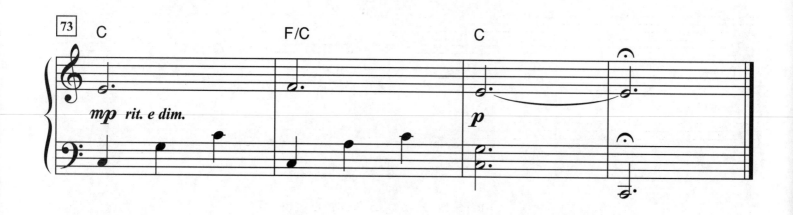

mp rit. e dim.

p

BIG YELLOW TAXI

Joni Mitchell was inspired to write "Big Yellow Taxi" after taking a trip to Hawaii. In an interview she said that she arrived in Hawaii at night, woke up the next morning, and looked out of her hotel room window at the beautiful, tropical landscape. A second glance directed her attention to the hotel's parking lot, and sparked her thinking about the abuse of the environment. In 2002, Counting Crows covered the song with Vanessa Carlton singing backup vocals; it became one of their biggest hits.

Words and Music by Joni Mitchell
Arranged by Dan Coates

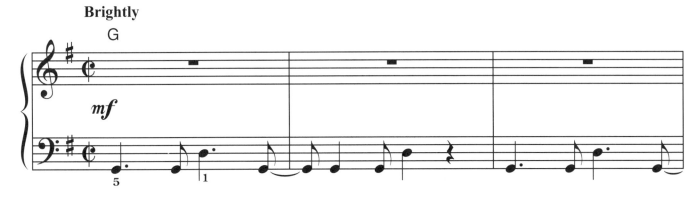

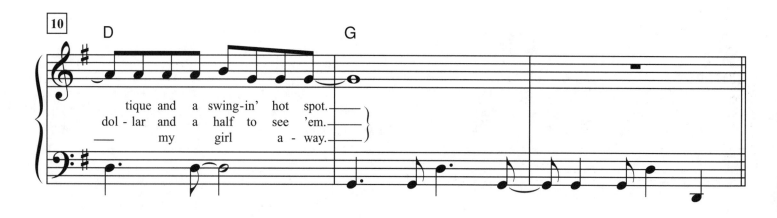

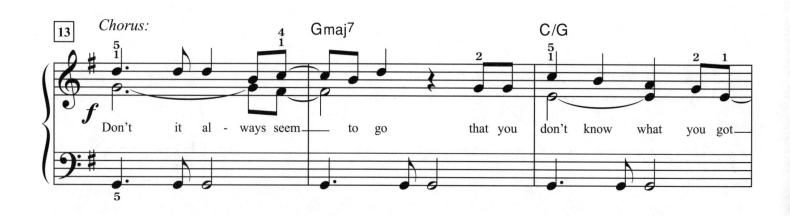

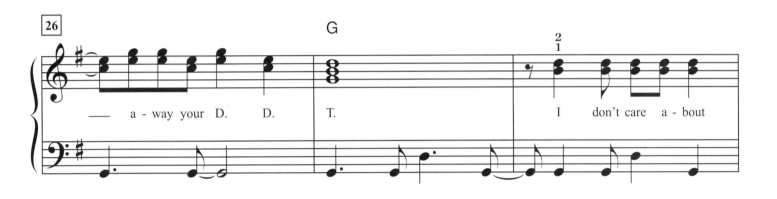

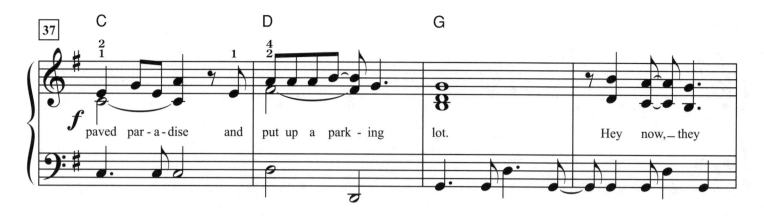

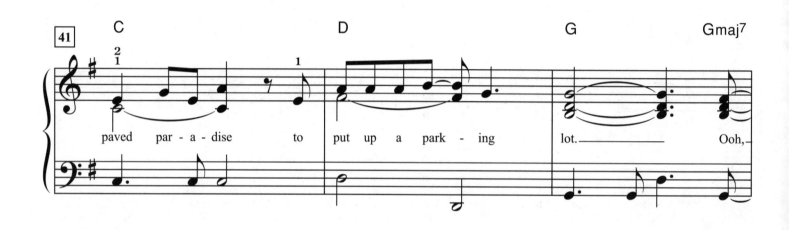

don't know what you got—— till it's gone. They paved par-a-dise and put up a park-ing

lot.————— Hey,— hey, hey.— They paved par-a-dise to put up a park-ing

cresc.

lot.————— Ooh,— bop bop.— They paved par-a-dise and put up a park-ing

ff

lot.—————

f   *rit.*

THE BEST OF MY LOVE

The Eagles recorded "The Best of My Love" in 1974 on their third studio album *On the Border*. The song, with lead vocals by Don Henley, would become the band's first of five #1 singles and helped pave the way to the Eagles becoming the best-selling American music group ever.

Words and Music by Don Henley,
Glenn Frey and John David Souther
Arranged by Dan Coates

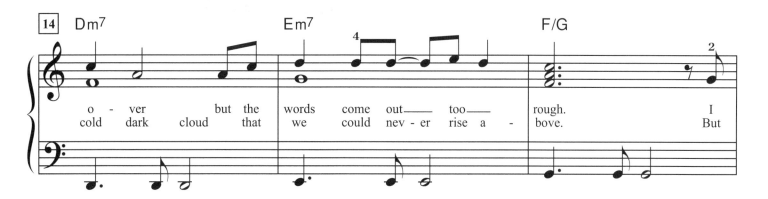

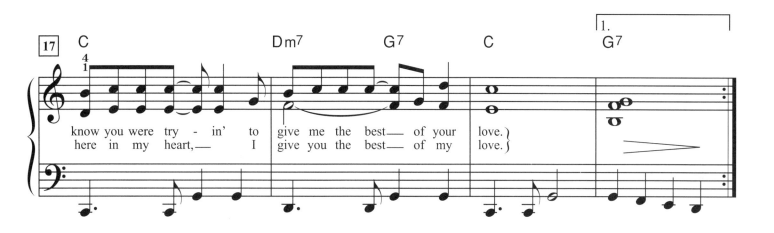

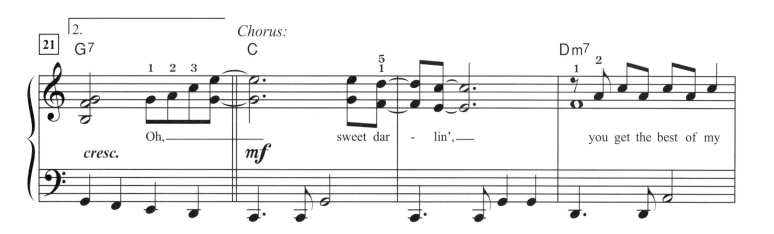

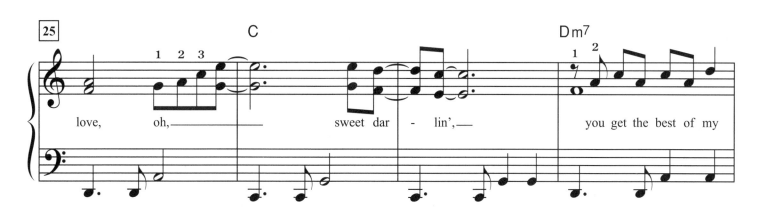

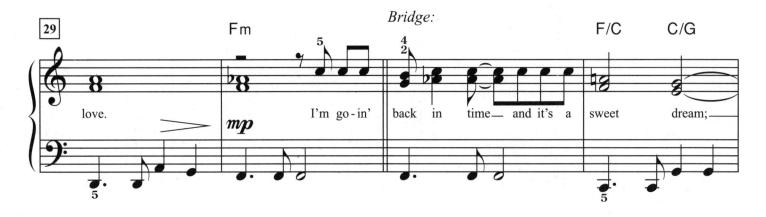

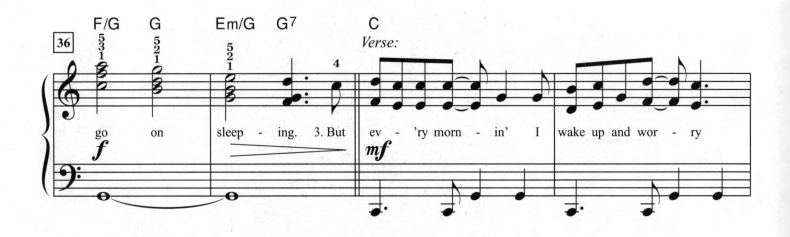

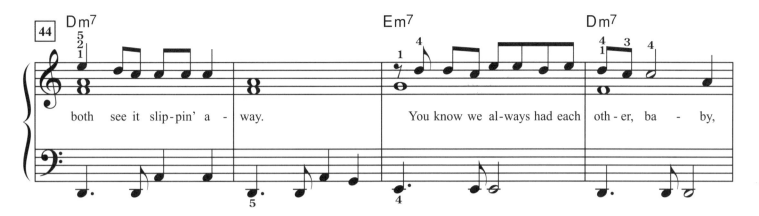

both see it slip-pin' a - way. You know we al-ways had each oth - er, ba - by,

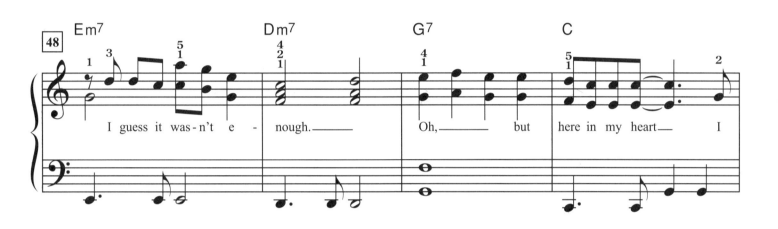

I guess it was-n't e - nough. Oh, but here in my heart I

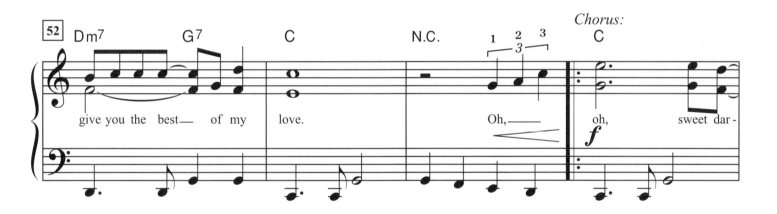

give you the best of my love. Oh, oh, sweet dar-

Chorus:

lin' you get the best of my love. Oh,

BRIDGE OVER TROUBLED WATER

Paul Simon and Art Garfunkel met in elementary school and performed in the same production of *Alice in Wonderland*. Years later they would collaborate as the duo Simon and Garfunkel and became known for their close vocal harmony, a sound reminiscent of The Everly Brothers. "Bridge Over Troubled Water" was their fifth and final studio album, which won five Grammy Awards. The title song stayed at the top of the Billboard Hot 100 for six weeks.

Words and Music by Paul Simon
Arranged by Dan Coates

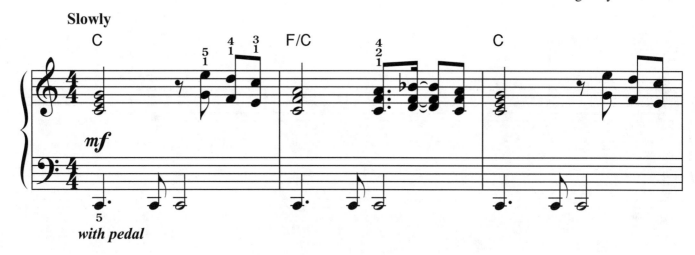

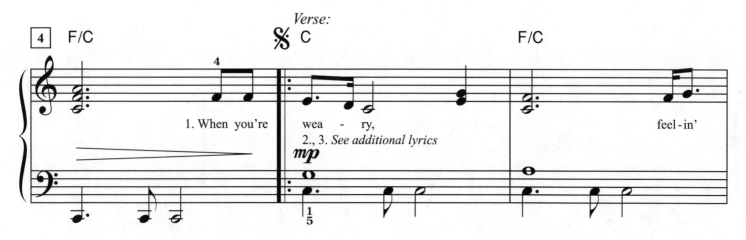

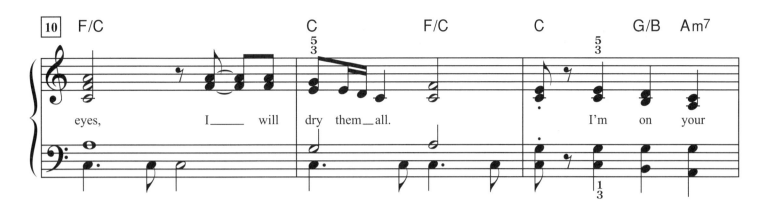

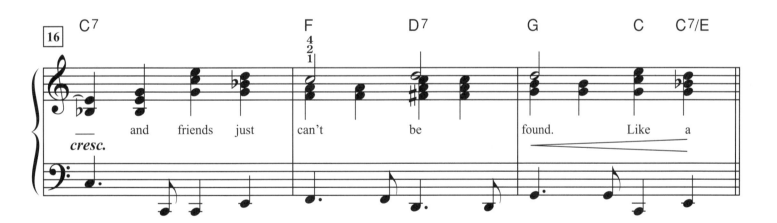

Chorus:

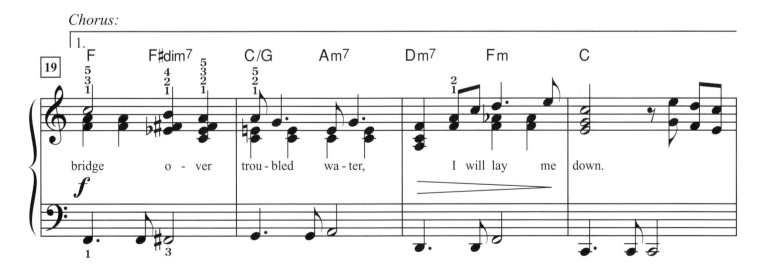

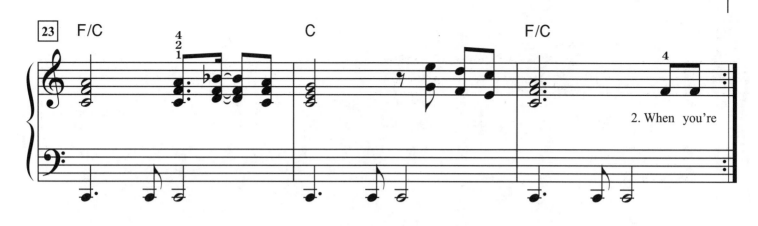

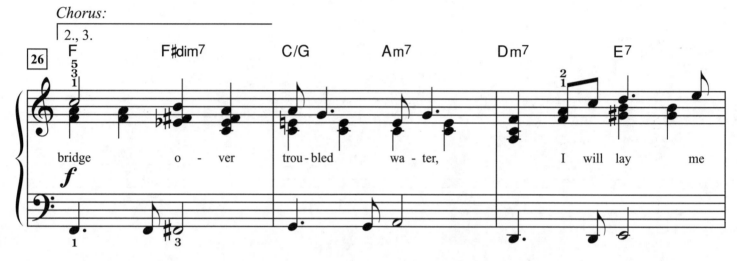

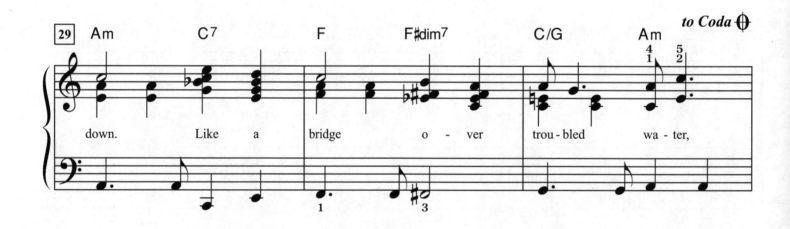

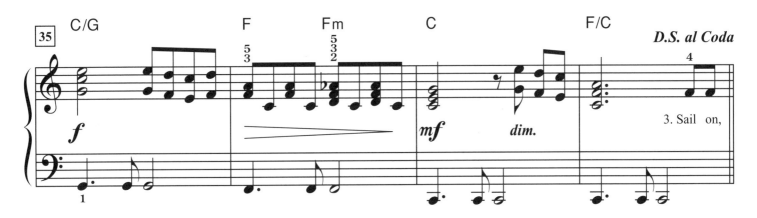

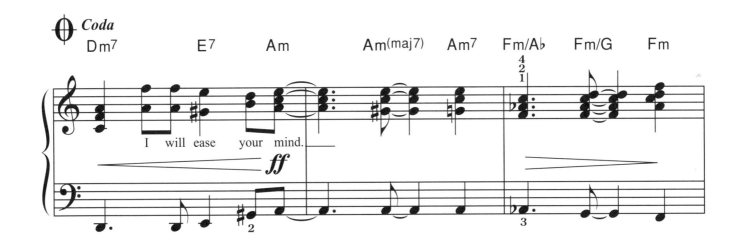

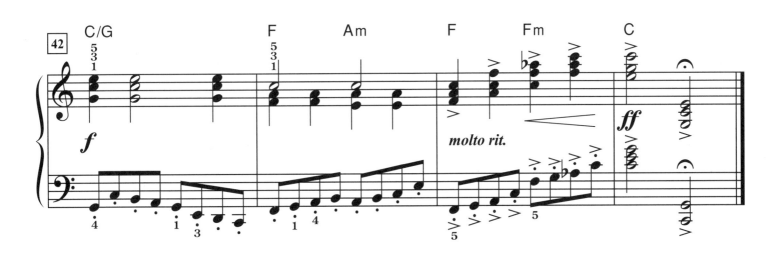

Verse 2:
When you're down and out,
When you're on the street,
When evening falls so hard, I will comfort you.
I'll take your part when darkness comes
And pain is all around.
Like a bridge over troubled water, I will lay me down.
Like a bridge over troubled water, I will lay me down.

Verse 3:
Sail on, silver girl, sail on by.
Your time has come to shine,
All your dreams are on their way.
See how they shine, if you need a friend.
I'm sailing right behind.
Like a bridge over troubled water, I will ease your mind.
Like a bridge over troubled water, I will ease your mind.

CAN YOU READ MY MIND?
(Love Theme from "Superman")

"Can You Read My Mind" is the love theme from the 1978 film *Superman*, starring Christopher Reeves (Superman), Marlon Brando (Jor-El), Gene Hackman (Lex Luthor), and Margot Kidder (Lois Lane). The song was recorded as a single, following the film's release, by Maureen McGovern.

Words by Leslie Bricusse
Music by **JOHN WILLIAMS**
Arranged by Dan Coates

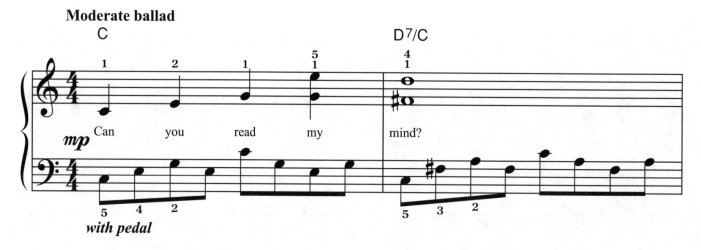

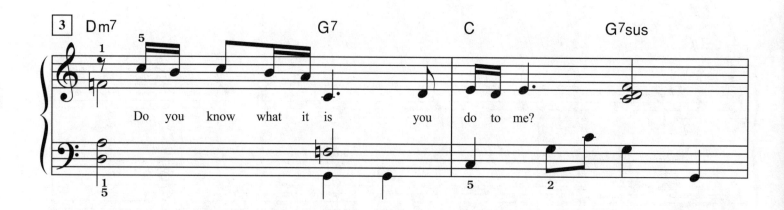

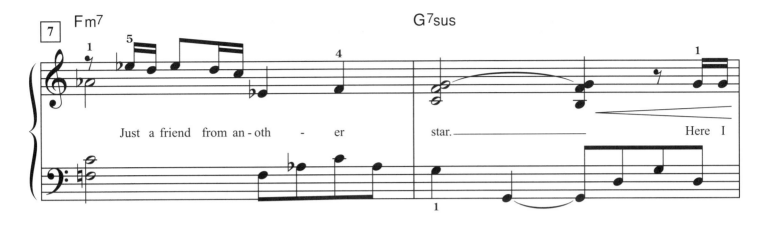

Just a friend from an-oth - er star. _____ Here I

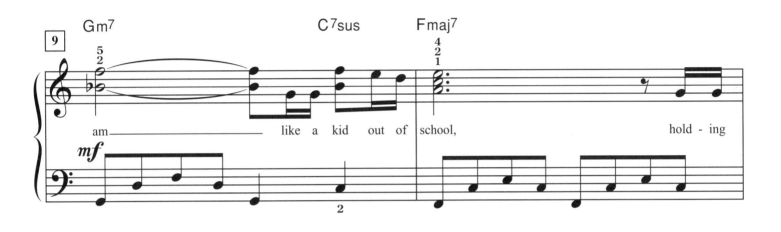

am _____ like a kid out of school, hold - ing

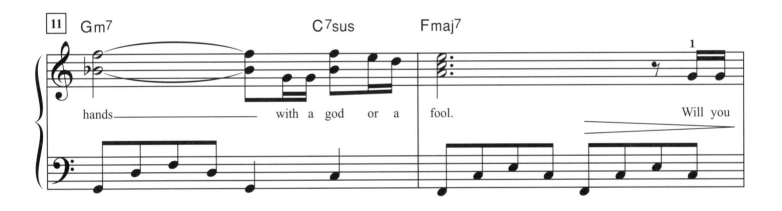

hands _____ with a god or a fool. Will you

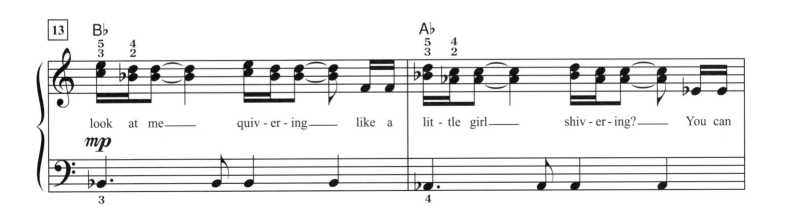

look at me _____ quiv-er-ing _____ like a lit-tle girl _____ shiv-er-ing? _____ You can

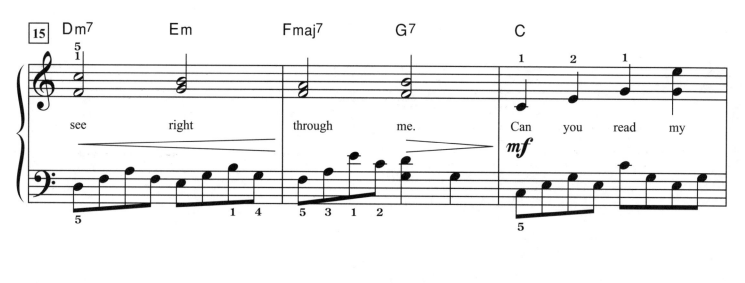

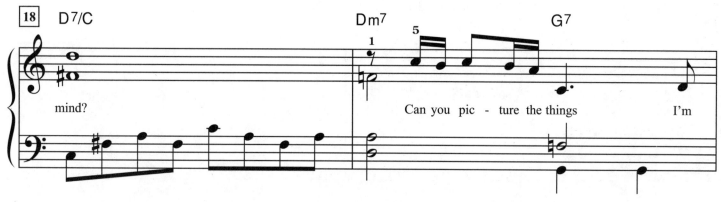

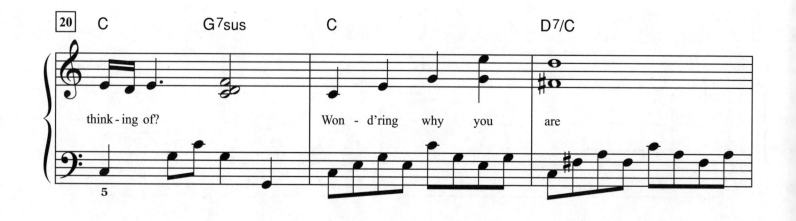

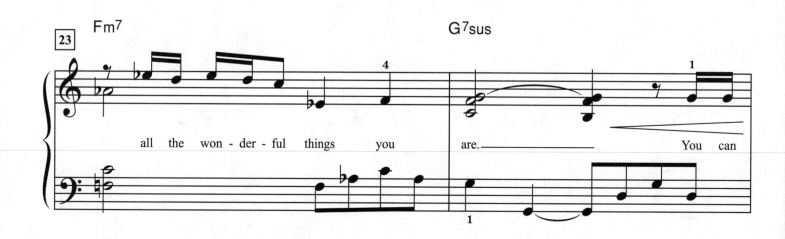

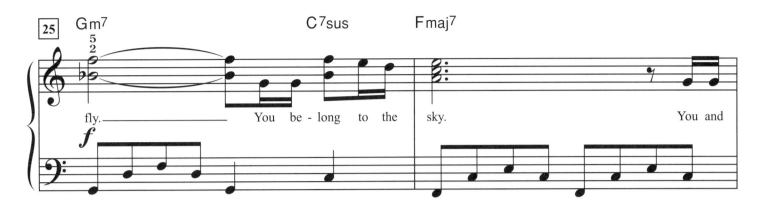

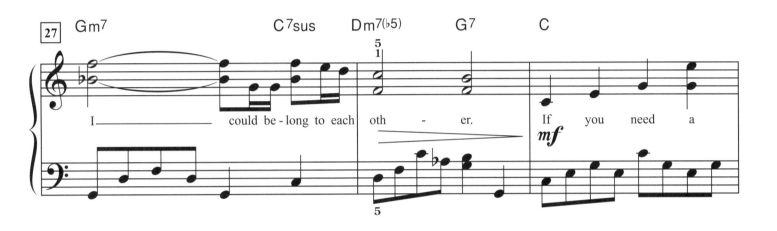

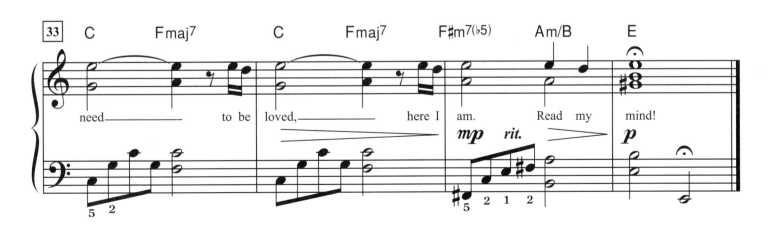

DANCING QUEEN

In 1975 the Swedish pop group, ABBA (an acronym for the first letters of the band members' names), recorded "Dancing Queen" on their album *Arrival*. It was released as a single the following year, reached the top of the charts internationally, and has become their signature song. Their pop/disco sound is quintessential of the '70s and can also be heard in their other hits: "Take a Chance on Me," "Super Trouper," and "S.O.S." to name a few.

Words and Music by Benny Andersson,
Stig Anderson and Bjorn Ulvaeus
Arranged by Dan Coates

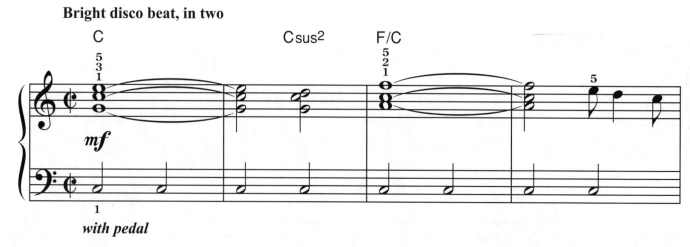

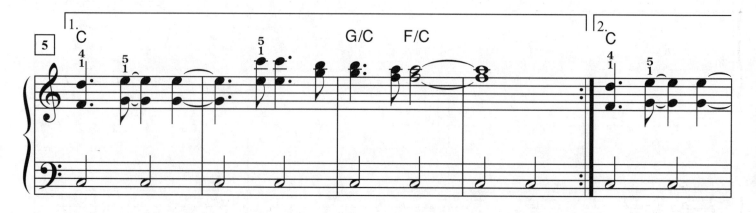

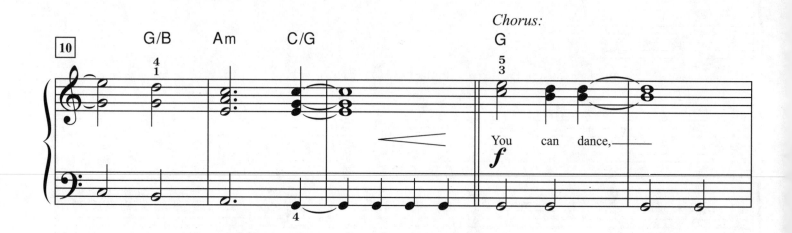

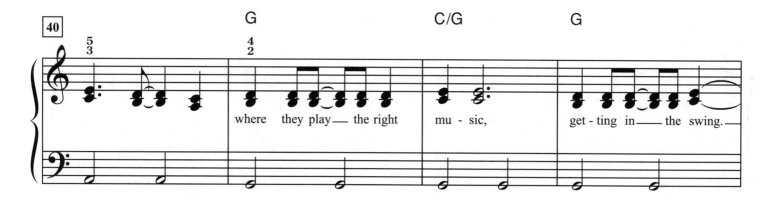

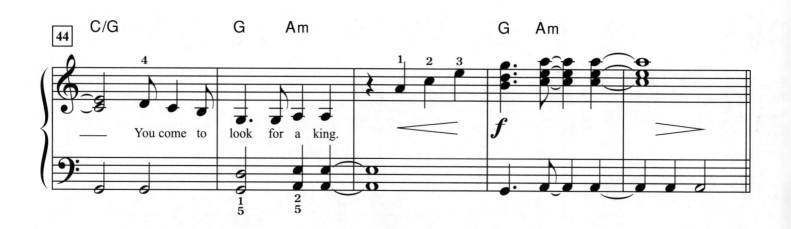

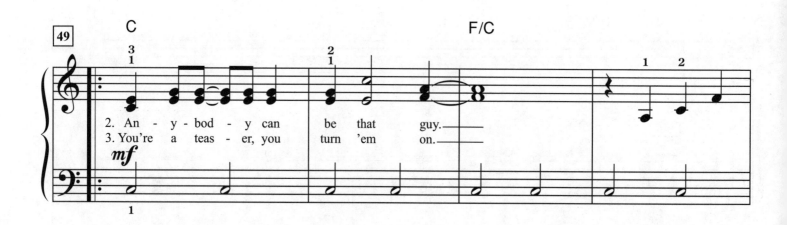

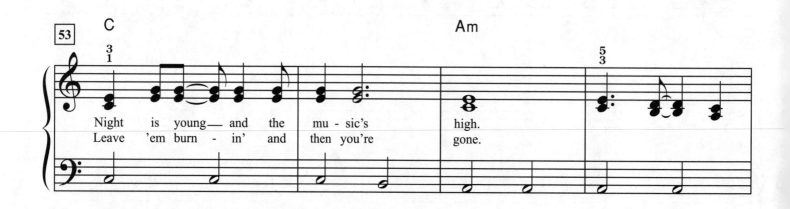

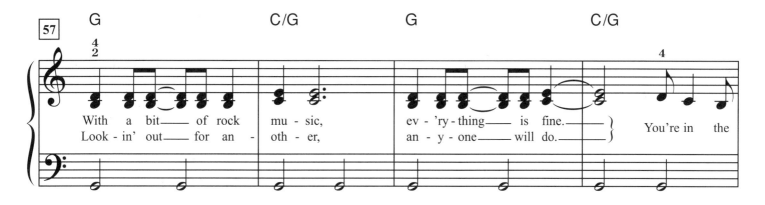

With a bit___ of rock   mu - sic,   ev - 'ry - thing___ is fine.___   You're in the
Look - in' out___ for an -   oth - er,   an - y - one___ will do.___

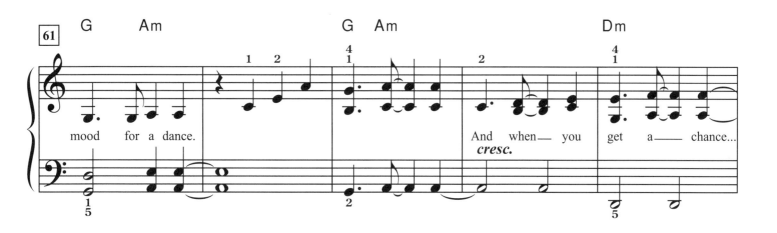

mood   for a dance.   And when___ you   get a___ chance...
cresc.

Chorus:

You   are___ the   danc - ing___ queen.___
f

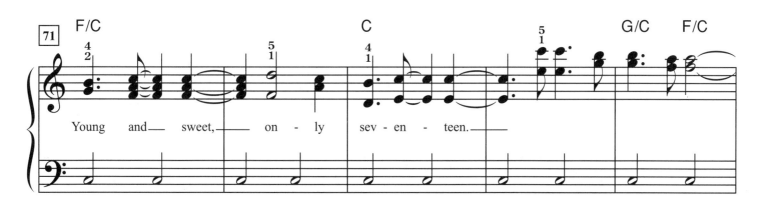

Young   and___ sweet,___   on - ly   sev - en - teen.___

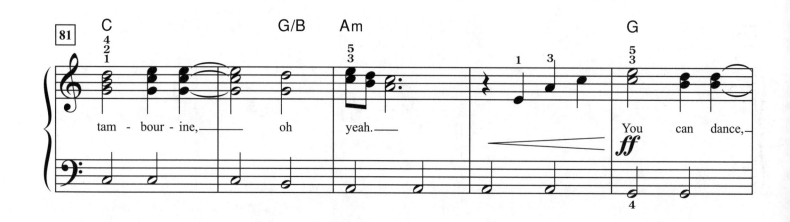

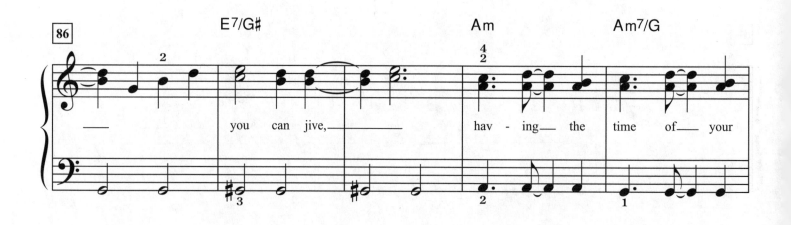

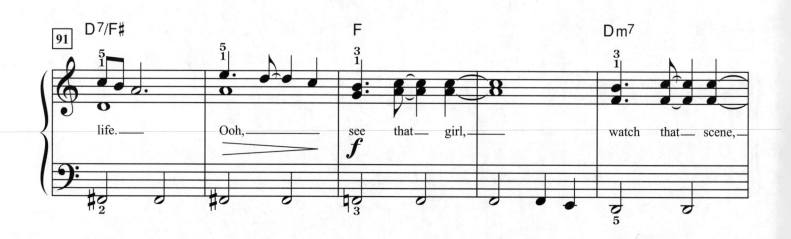

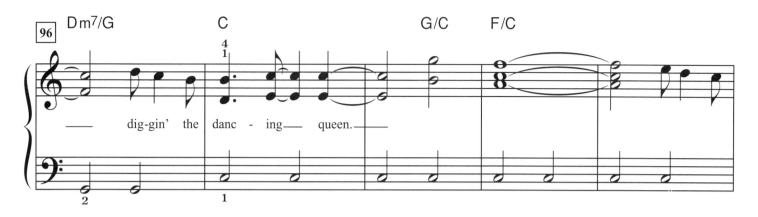

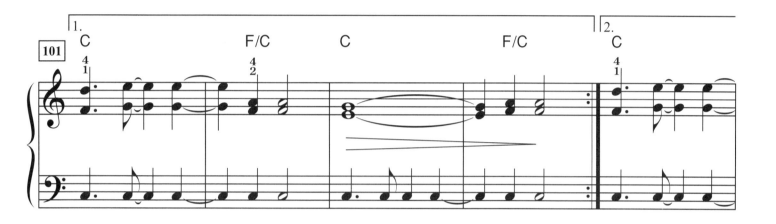

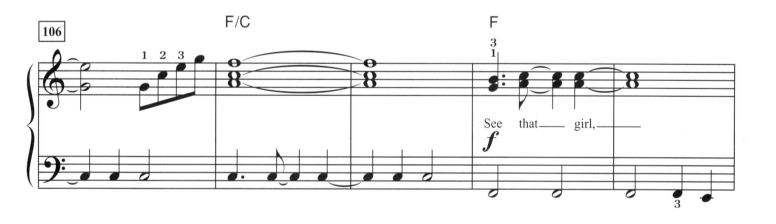

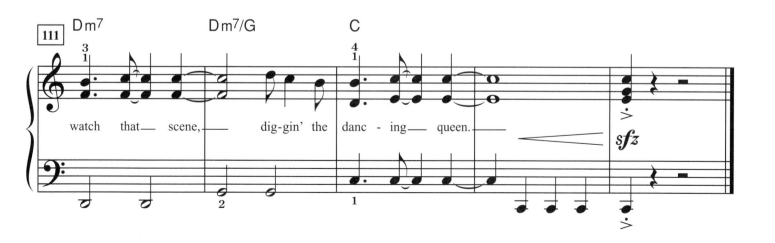

DESPERADO

"Desperado" first appeared on the 1973 Eagles album of the same name. *Desperado* was a concept album based on the Dalton Gang, outlaws of the Old West. Although "Desperado" was never released as a single, it has become one of their signature songs. It also has been covered by numerous artists including Linda Ronstadt, The Carpenters, Clint Black, Johnny Cash, Carrie Underwood, and The Dixie Chicks.

Words and Music by
Don Henley and Glenn Frey
Arranged by Dan Coates

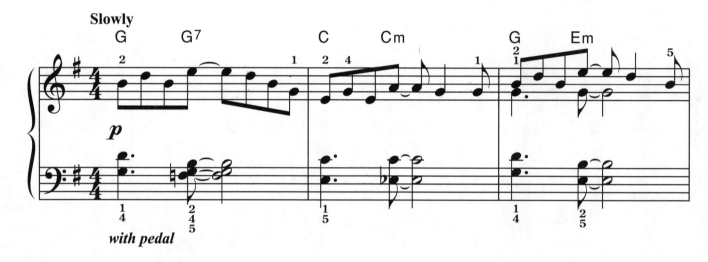

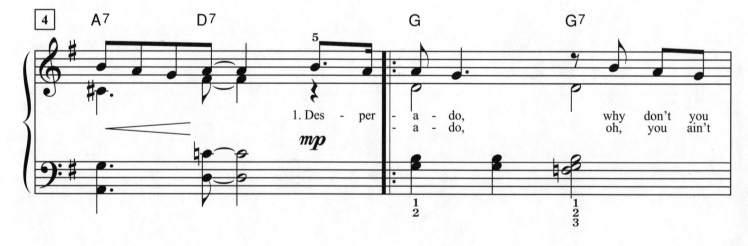

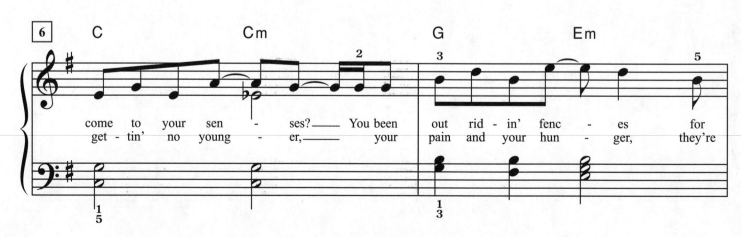

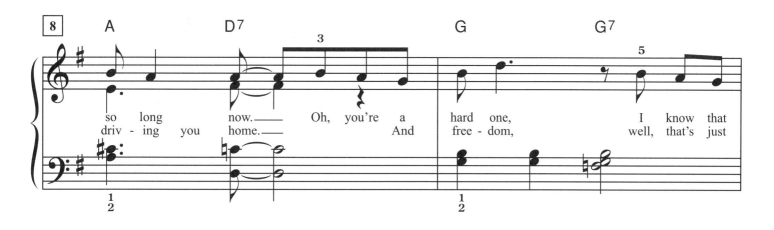

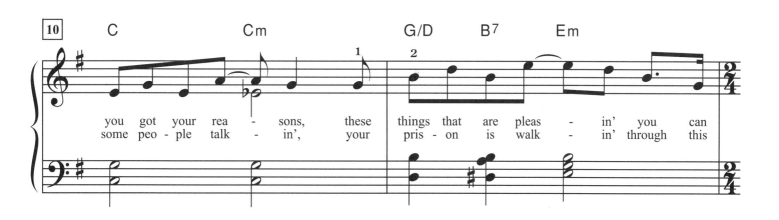

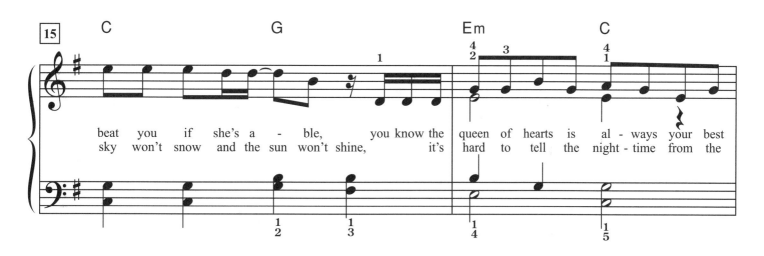

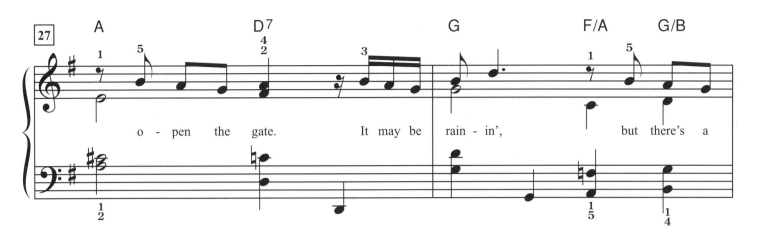

o - pen the gate. It may be rain - in', but there's a

rain - bow a - bove you.＿ You bet - ter let some - bod - y - love＿ you,

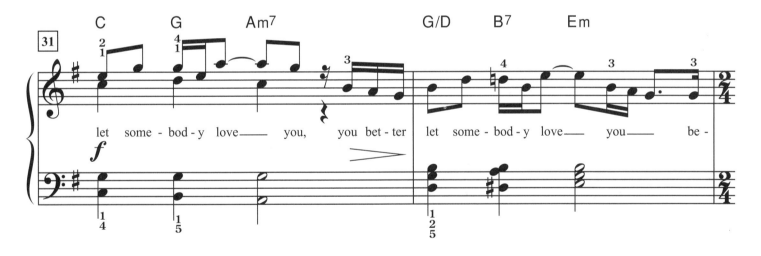

let some - bod - y love＿ you, you bet - ter let some - bod - y love＿ you＿ be -

fore it's too late.

DON'T IT MAKE MY BROWN EYES BLUE

Crystal Gayle was the first female country singer to have a platinum album with her release of "Don't It Make My Brown Eyes Blue." The 1977 song was written by Richard Leigh. In an interview Crystal Gayle stated that the song was inspired by Leigh's dog; it had one brown eye and one blue eye.

Words and Music by Richard Leigh
Arranged by Dan Coates

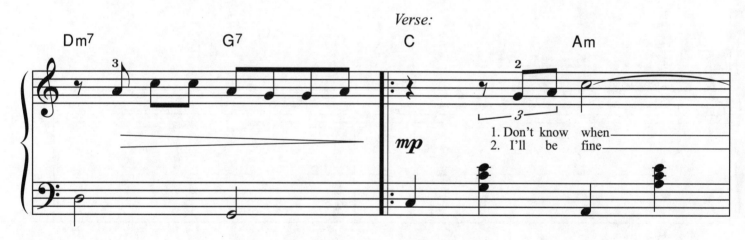

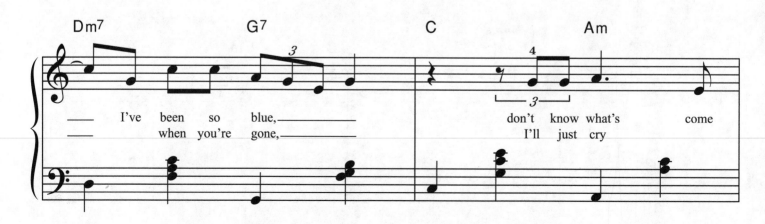

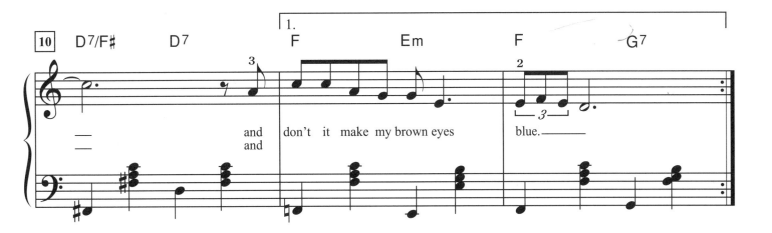

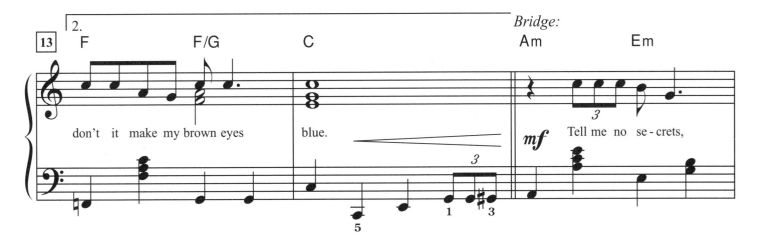

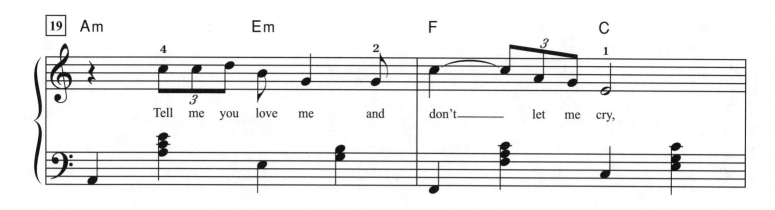

Tell me you love me and don't let me cry,

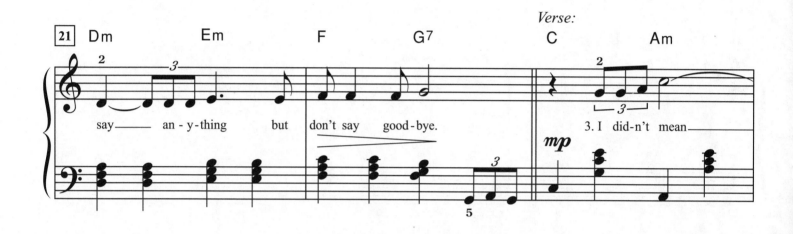

say anything but don't say good-bye.

3. I didn't mean

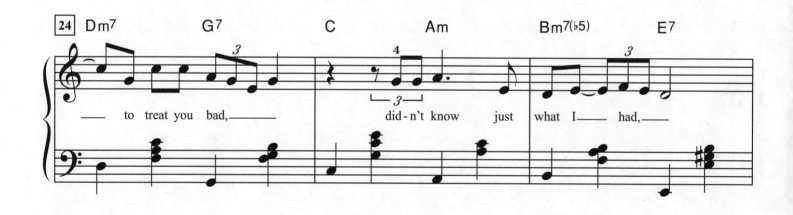

to treat you bad, didn't know just what I had,

but honey now I do and don't it make my brown eyes,

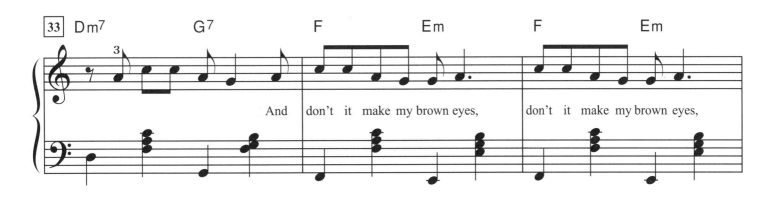

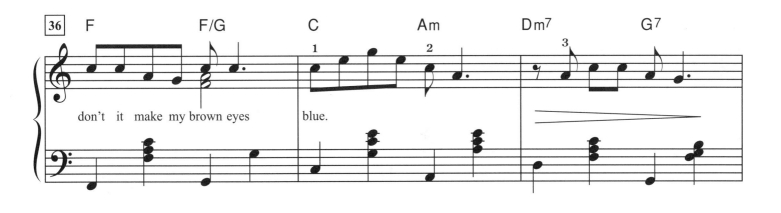

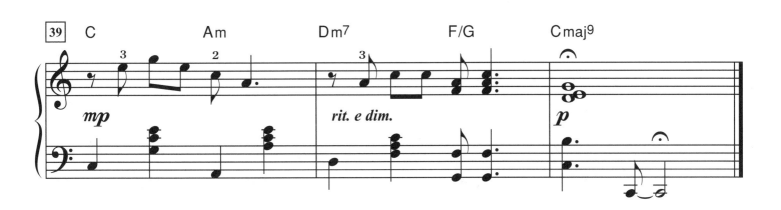

EASE ON DOWN THE ROAD

In 1975 *The Wiz* opened on Broadway and was the first musical to feature African American actors. It was an adaptation of L. Frank Baum's *The Wonderful Wizard of Oz*, the same children's novel that inspired MGM's classic film *The Wizard of Oz*. "Ease on Down the Road" is an R & B re-interpretation of "Follow the Yellow Brick Road" and "We're Off to See the Wizard." It is most famously known as the duet sung by Diana Ross and Michael Jackson in the film adaptation.

Words and Music by Charlie Smalls
Arranged by Dan Coates

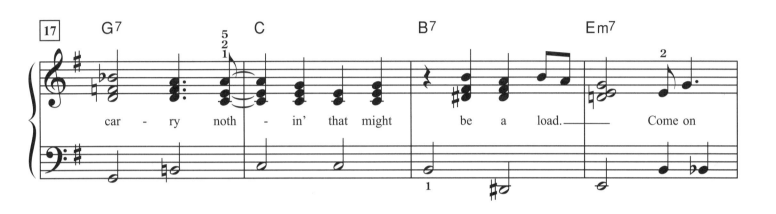

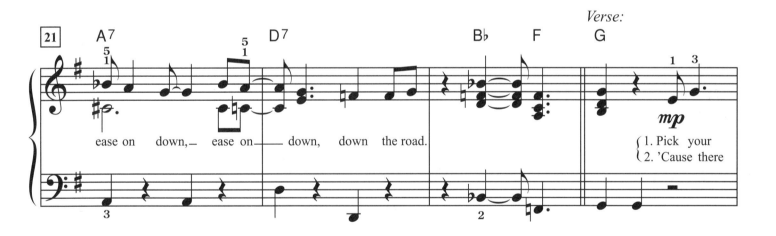

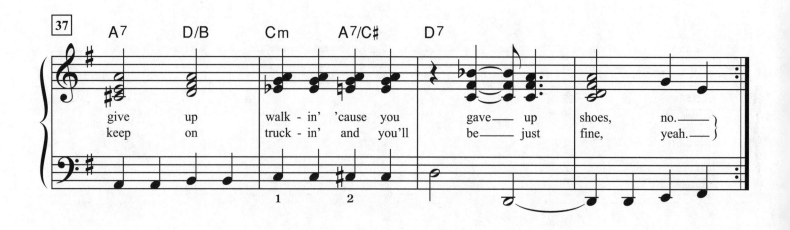

Chorus:

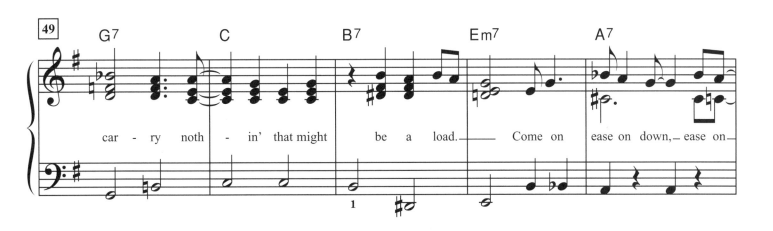

EVERGREEN
(Love Theme from "A Star Is Born")

"Evergreen" was a worldwide success in 1976, peaking at #1 on the Billboard Hot 100 and winning Academy, Grammy, and Golden Globe awards. It was composed and performed by Barbra Streisand for the film *A Star Is Born*, starring Streisand and Kris Kristofferson. It is a story about a couple whose unequally successful singing careers create drama in their relationship. The movie is a remake of two earlier versions—one starring Janet Gaynor (1937) and one starring Judy Garland (1954).

Words by Paul Williams
Music by Barbra Streisand
Arranged by Dan Coates

Moderately slow

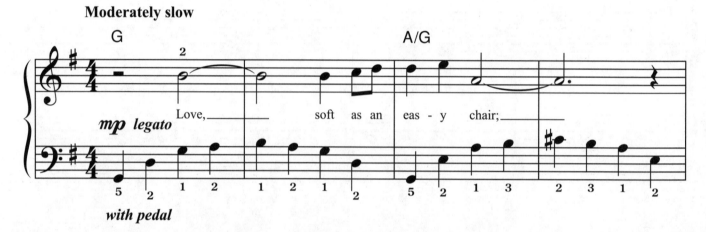

CHARLIE'S ANGELS
(Main Theme)

Kate Jackson, Farrah Fawcett-Majors, and Jaclyn Smith were the original "angels" in the ABC series *Charlie's Angels*. The show ran from 1976 to 1981 and featured the three women as undercover private investigators who would receive their assignments from their boss, Charlie, via speakerphone. The show inspired two feature films, video games, collectibles, and even an increase in the use of the name "Charlie."

By Jack Elliott and Allyn M. Ferguson
Arranged by Dan Coates

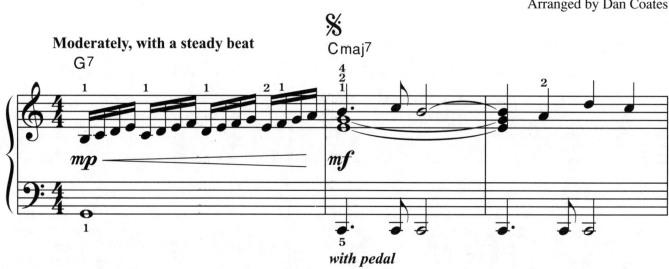

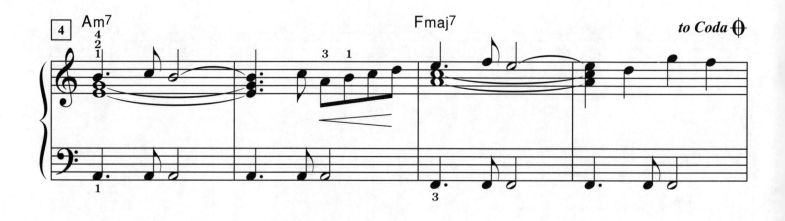

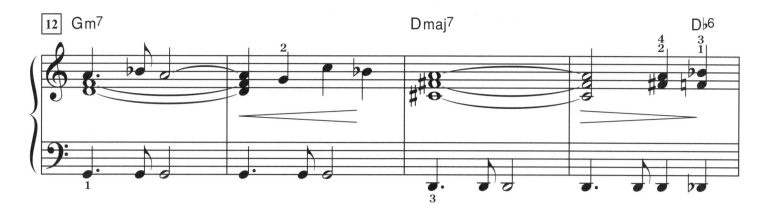

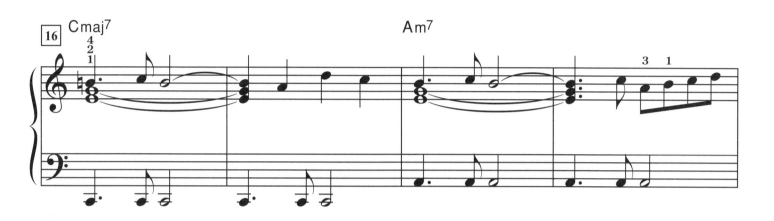

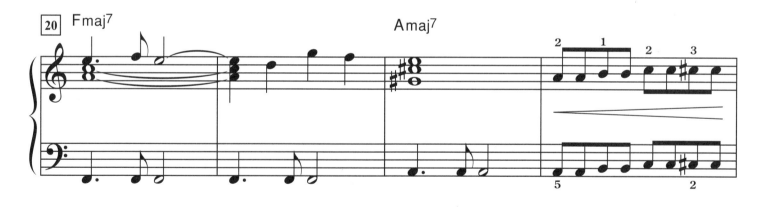

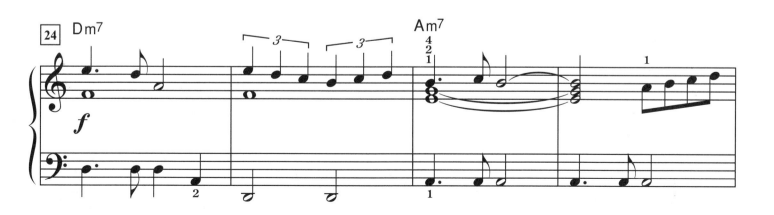

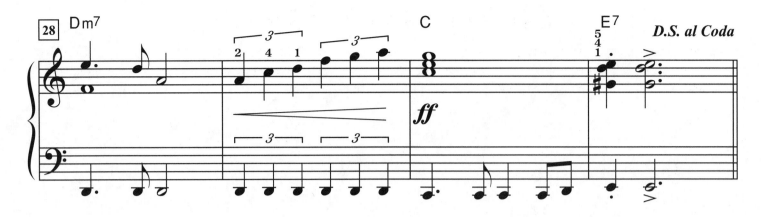

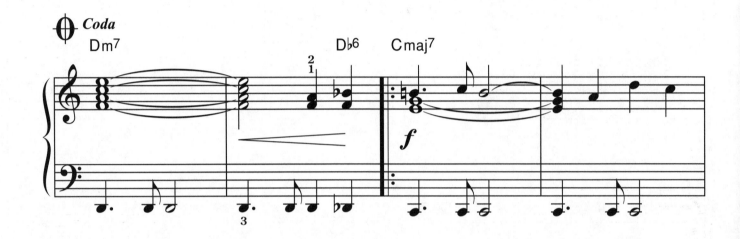

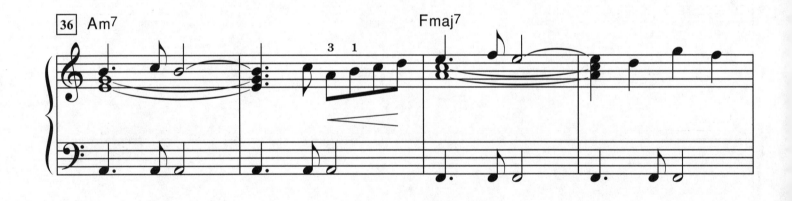

GO YOUR OWN WAY

Fleetwood Mac released their album *Rumours* in 1977. It became the best-selling album of the year and spent six months at the top of the U.S. charts and won the Grammy Award for Album of the Year. There were a number of hit singles on the album including "Dreams," "Don't Stop," "You Make Loving Fun," and "Go Your Own Way."

Words and Music by Lindsey Buckingham
Arranged by Dan Coates

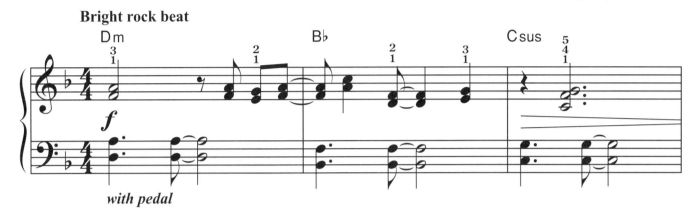

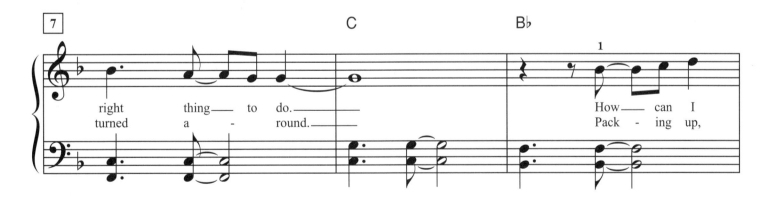

If____ I could, may - be I'd give____ you____ my world.
If____ I could, ba - by, I'd give____ you____ my world.

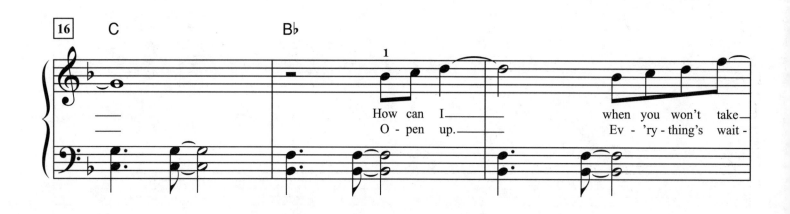

How can I____ when you won't take____
O - pen up.____ Ev - 'ry - thing's wait -

Chorus:

____ it from____ me?
ing for____ you.

You can go____

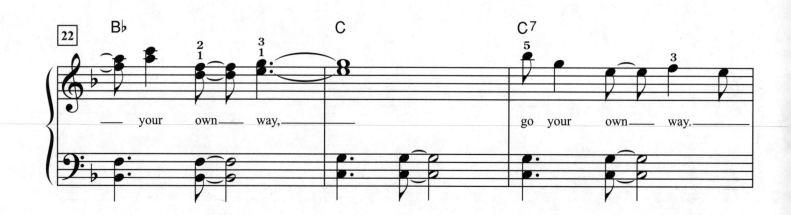

____ your own____ way,____ go your own____ way.____

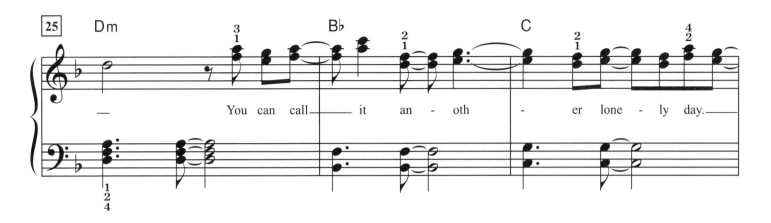

You can call it an - oth - er lone - ly day.

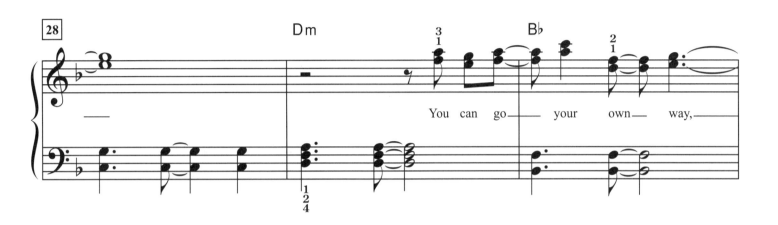

You can go your own way,

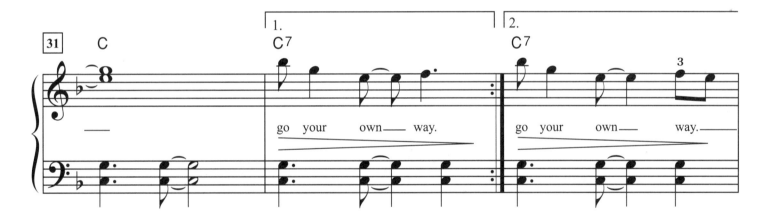

go your own way.

go your own way.

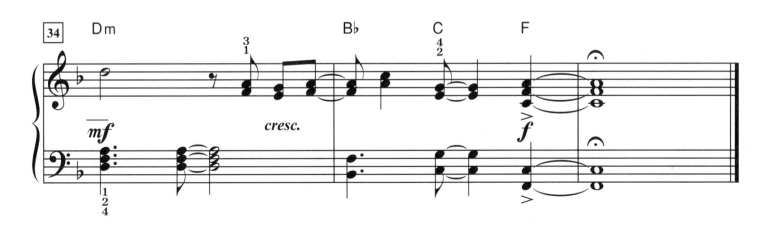

mf *cresc.* *f*

THE GREATEST LOVE OF ALL

George Benson recorded "The Greatest Love of All" for *The Greatest*, a 1977 film which starred boxing legend Muhammad Ali as himself. Linda Creed wrote the lyrics amidst a struggle with breast cancer; the words reflect her feelings about coping with the disease and being a young mother. Whitney Houston covered the song in 1986 on her self-titled debut album, a record which would eventually sell over 13 million copies and become one of the best-selling female debut albums in history.

Words by Linda Creed
Music by Michael Masser
Arranged by Dan Coates

Slowly, with expression

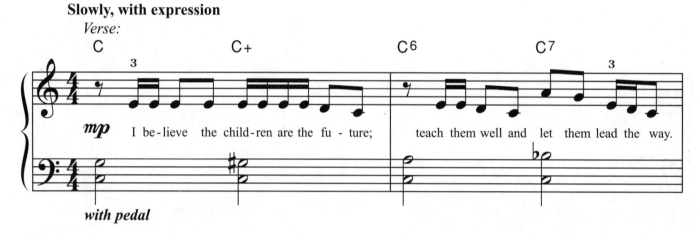

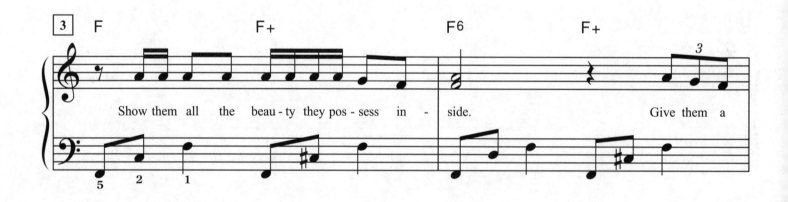

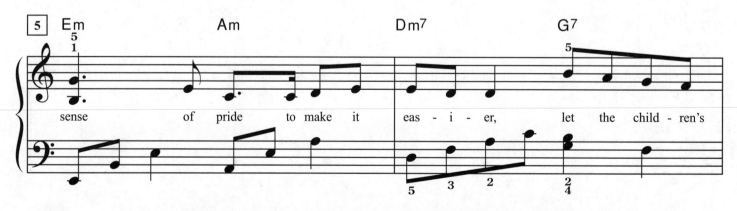

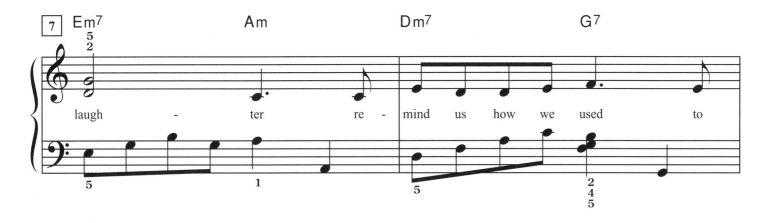

7 | Em7 ... Am ... Dm7 ... G7

laugh - ter re - mind us how we used to

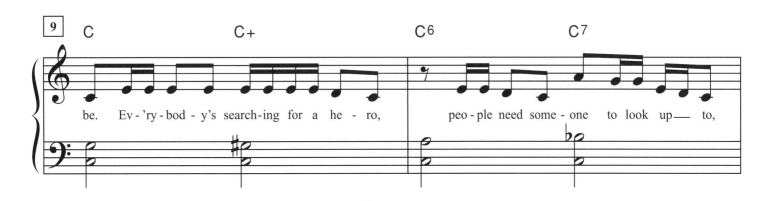

9 | C ... C+ ... C6 ... C7

be. Ev - 'ry - bod - y's search-ing for a he - ro, peo - ple need some - one to look up — to,

11 | F ... F+ ... F6 ... F+

I nev - er found an - y - one who ful - filled that need; a lone - ly

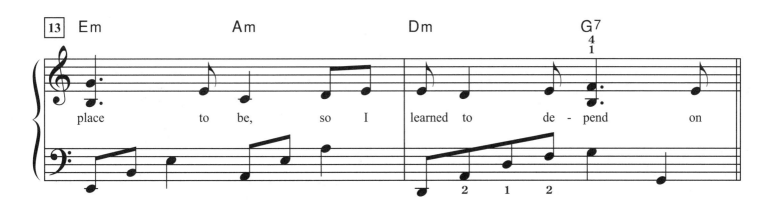

13 | Em ... Am ... Dm ... G7

place to be, so I learned to de - pend on

Bridge:

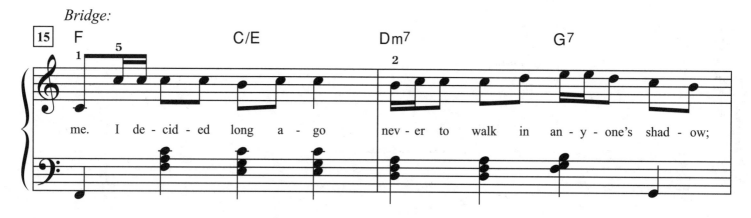

15 F   C/E   Dm7   G7

me. I de - cid - ed long a - go   nev - er to walk in an - y - one's shad - ow;

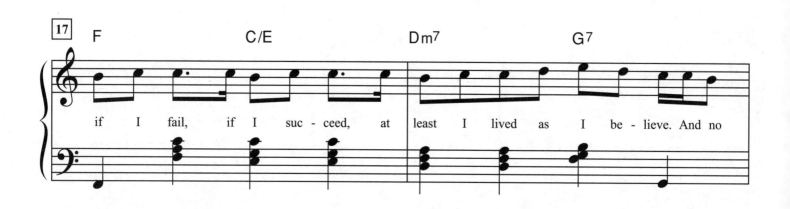

17 F   C/E   Dm7   G7

if I fail, if I suc - ceed, at   least I lived as I be - lieve. And no

19 F   C/E   Dm7   G7

mat - ter what they take from me, they   can't take a - way my dig - ni - ty.   Be - cause the

cresc.

Chorus:

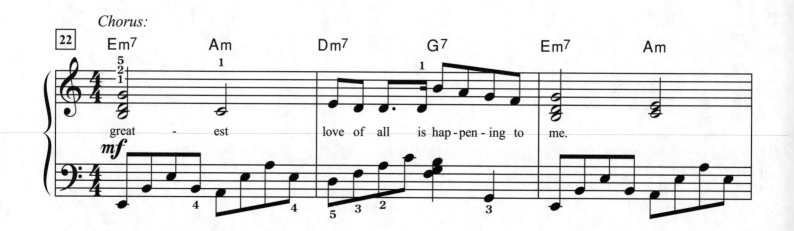

22 Em7   Am   Dm7   G7   Em7   Am

great - est   love of all is hap - pen - ing to me.

mf

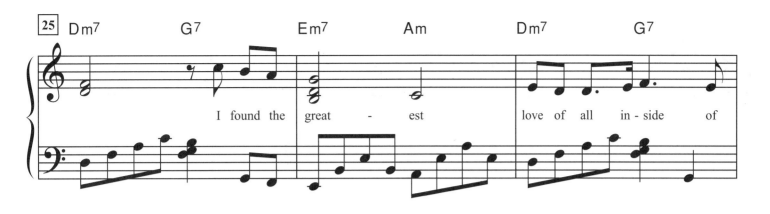

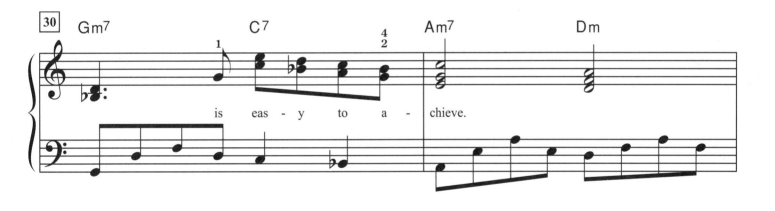

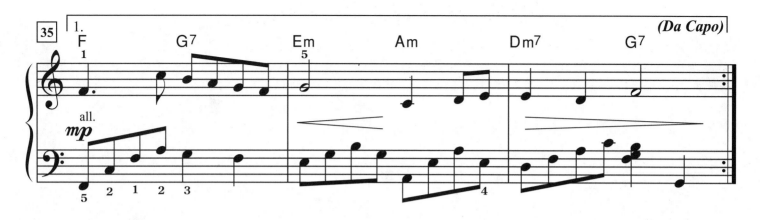

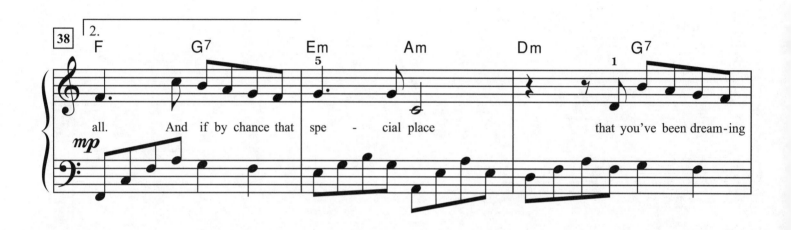

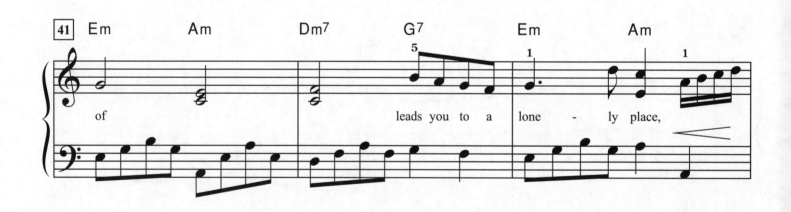

HOTEL CALIFORNIA

Hotel California was released by the Eagles in 1976 and was the first Eagles album without founding member Bernie Leadon. Since then it has sold over 16 million copies in the U.S. alone. The album was #1 on the Billboard 200 for eight weeks in 1977 and has become one of the top 15 best-selling albums of all time in any category.

Words and Music by Don Henley,
Glenn Frey, and Don Felder
Arranged by Dan Coates

Up a - head in the dis - tance, I saw a shim - mer - ing light.
How they dance in the court - yard; sweet sum - mer sweat.

My head grew heav - y and my sight grew dim; I had to stop for the night.__
Some dance to re - mem - ber; some dance to for - get.__

There she stood in the door - way; I heard the mis - sion bell.__
So I called up the cap - tain: "Please bring me my wine." He said,

And I was think - ing to my - self:__ this could be heav - en or this could be hell.____
"We have-n't had that spir - it here__ since nine - teen six - ty - nine."__

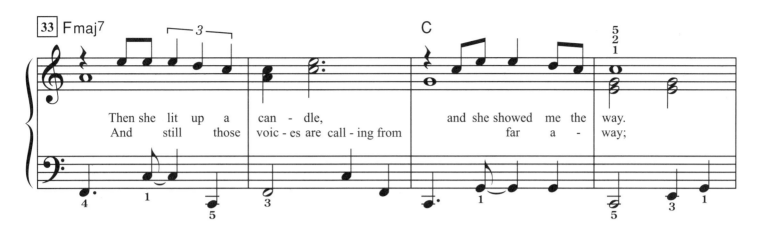

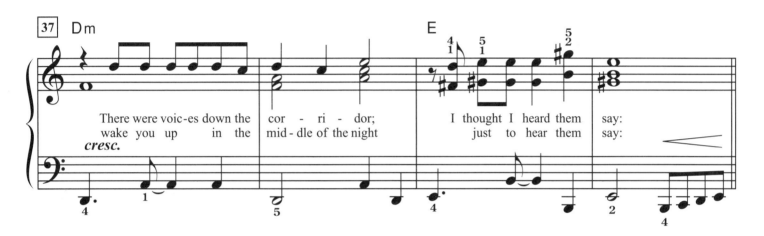

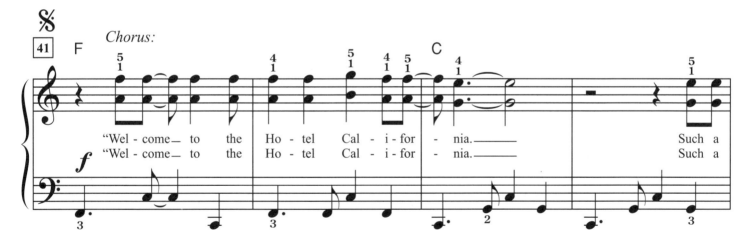

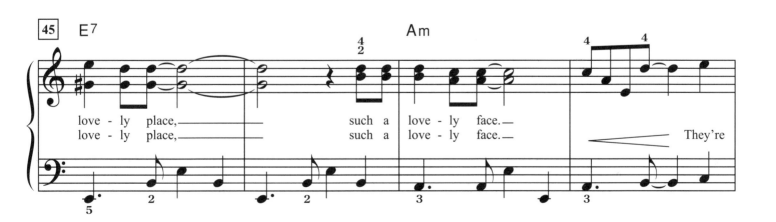

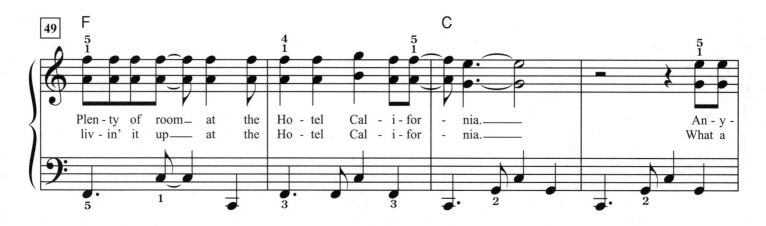

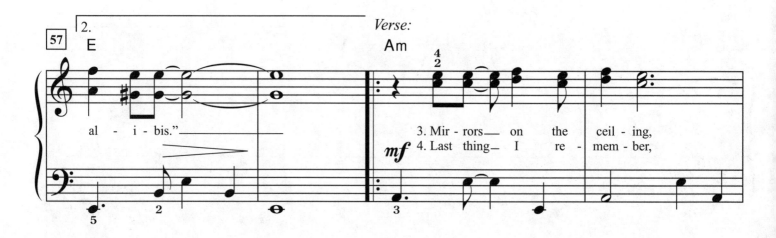

pris - on - ers here
pas - sage back to the

of our own— de - vice."
place I was— be - fore.

And in the mas - ter's—
"Re - lax," said the

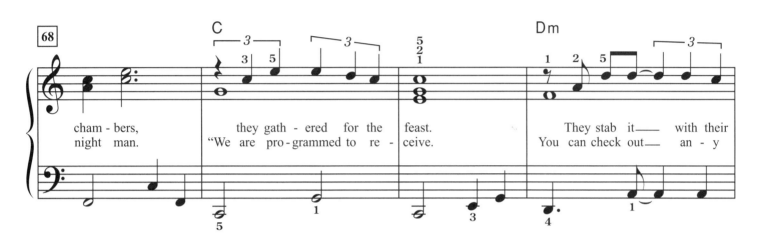

cham - bers,
night man.

they gath - ered for the feast.
"We are pro - grammed to re - ceive.

They stab it—— with their
You can check out— an - y

steel - y knives, but they
time you like, but

just can't— kill the beast.
you can— nev - er

1.

2.

D.S. al Coda

leave."

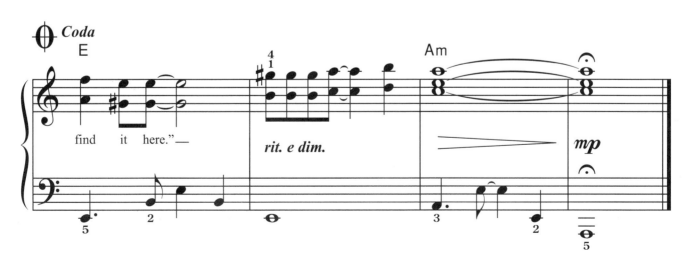

Coda

find it here."—

rit. e dim.

mp

KILLING ME SOFTLY WITH HIS SONG

"Killing Me Softly with His Song" was written in 1971 and inspired by a poem by Lori Lieberman ("Killing Me Softly with His Blues") which she wrote after witnessing a live performance by Don McLean, the gifted folk rock singer who would later release the big hit "American Pie." Roberta Flack covered "Killing Me Softly with His Song" in 1973, a recording which won three Grammy Awards.

Words and Music by
Charles Fox and Norman Gimbel
Arranged by Dan Coates

LAYLA

"Layla" is the title track from Derek and the Dominos album *Layla and Other Assorted Love Songs* released in 1970. It was written by Eric Clapton and inspired by his then unrequited love for Pattie Boyd (who was married to George Harrison at the time) and also an Arabian love story ("The Story of Layla / Layla and Majnun") about a princess's arranged marriage.

Words and Music by
Eric Clapton and Jim Gordon
Arranged by Dan Coates

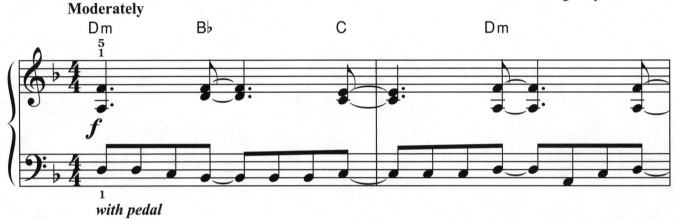

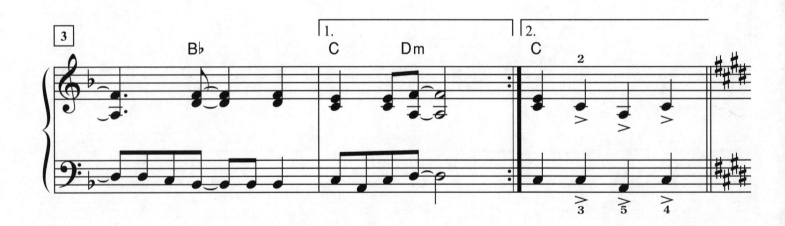

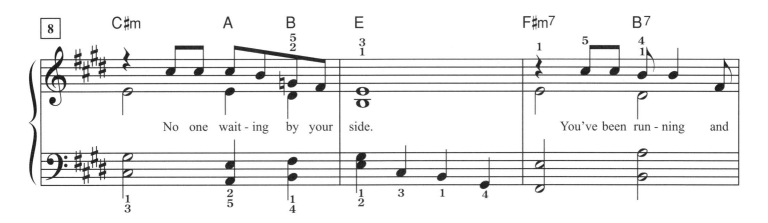

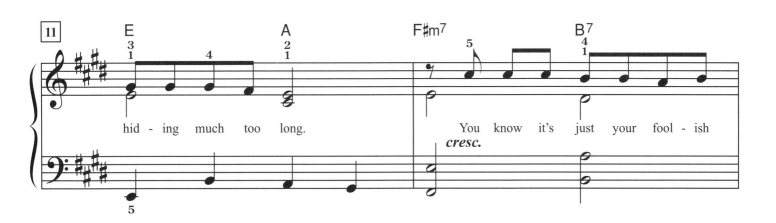

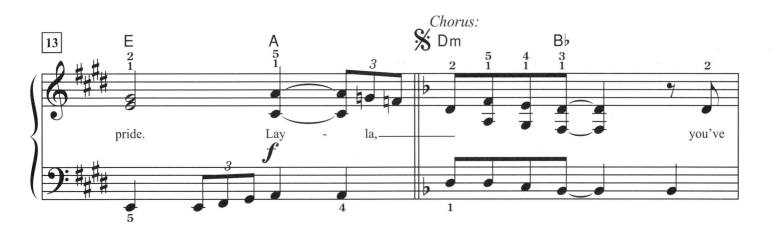

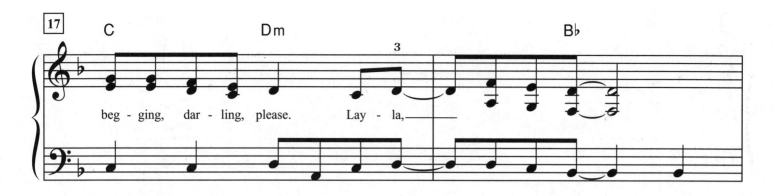

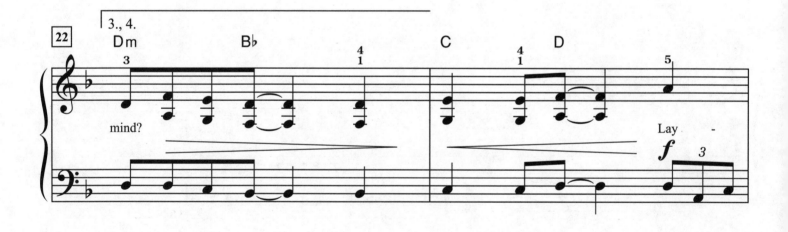

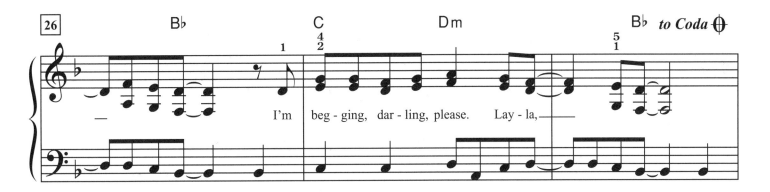

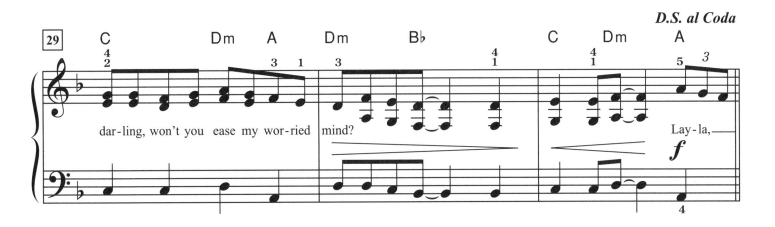

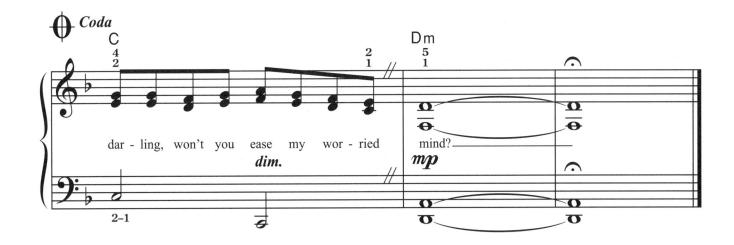

Verse 2:
Tried to give you consolation,
Your old man won't let you down.
Like a fool, I fell in love with you.
You turned my whole world upside down.
(To Chorus:)

Verse 3:
Make the best of the situation
Before I finally go insane.
Please don't say we'll never find a way
And tell me all my love's in vain.
(To Chorus:)

HOW DEEP IS YOUR LOVE

The Bee Gees recorded "How Deep Is Your Love" in 1977, and soon after the song rose to the top of the Billboard Charts staying in the top 10 for 17 weeks. It was used along with their other huge hit, "Stayin' Alive," in *Saturday Night Fever*, the John Travolta film that helped popularize disco music around the world.

Words and Music by Barry Gibb,
Maurice Gibb and Robin Gibb
Arranged by Dan Coates

Moderately, with a steady beat

LOVE STORY
(Where Do I Begin)

Love Story was released in 1970 and is one of the world's greatest romantic films. It starred Ali MacGraw (Jenny Cavilleri) and Ryan O'Neal (Oliver Barrett IV), a young couple who, like Romeo and Juliet, face a star-crossed love. Francis Lai won a Golden Globe and Academy Award for his score for the film, and the film's theme became a hit single sung by Andy Williams.

Lyrics by Carl Sigman
Music by Francis Lai
Arranged by Dan Coates

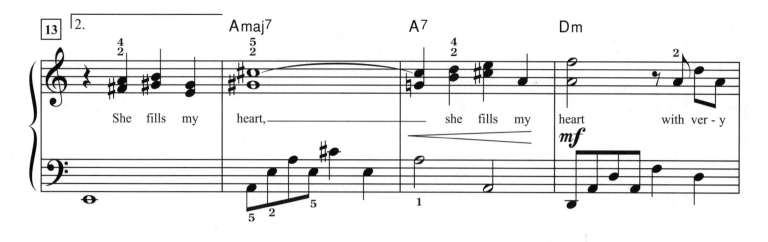

She fills my heart,_____ she fills my heart with ver - y

spe - cial things, with an - gel songs, with wild im - ag - in - ings. She fills my

soul with so much love that an - y - where I go I'm nev - er

lone - ly. With her a - long, who could be lone - ly? I reach for her

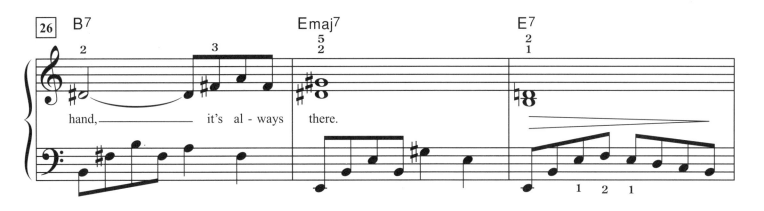

26 B7   Emaj7   E7

hand,_____ it's al - ways there.

29 Am   E7/G#

How long does it last? Can love be meas - ured by the hours____ in a day?

mp

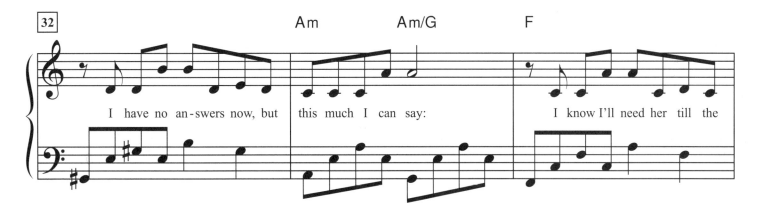

32   Am   Am/G   F

I have no an - swers now, but this much I can say: I know I'll need her till the

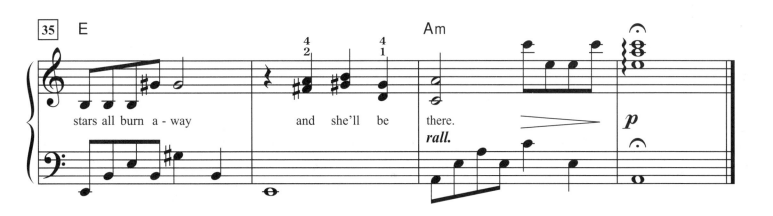

35 E   Am

stars all burn a - way and she'll be there.

rall.   *p*

MAGGIE MAY

Rod Stewart recorded "Maggie May" as a single in 1971. It was originally the B-side of the "Reason to Believe" single release, but was re-classified as the A-side after a tremendous public response. It climbed to the #1 position in the U.K. and topped the charts in the United States; Stewart's album *Every Picture Tells a Story* simultaneously accomplished the same feat.

Words and Music by
Rod Stewart and Martin Quittenton
Arranged by Dan Coates

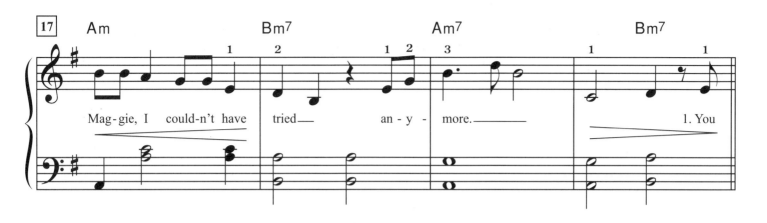

17 Am | Bm7 | Am7 | Bm7

Mag - gie, I could-n't have tried___ an - y - more.___ 1. You

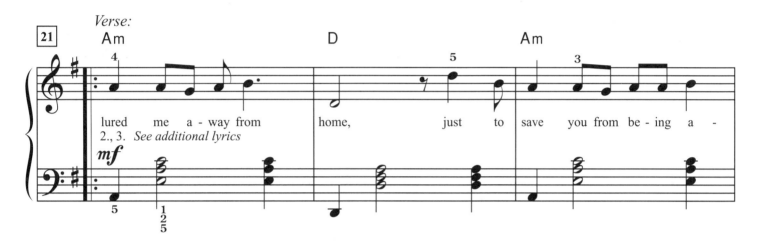

Verse:

21 Am | D | Am

lured me a - way from home, just to save you from be - ing a -

2., 3. *See additional lyrics*

mf

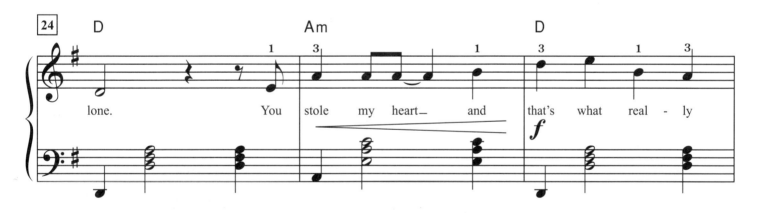

24 D | Am | D

lone. You stole my heart___ and that's what real - ly

f

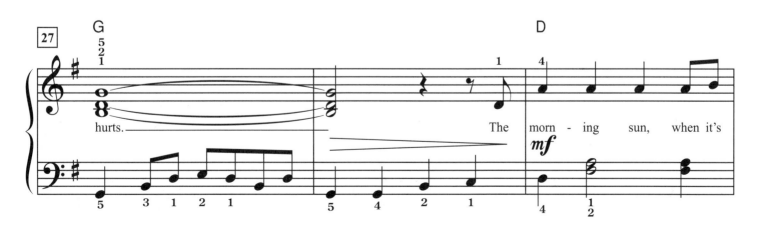

27 G | D

hurts.___ The morn - ing sun, when it's

mf

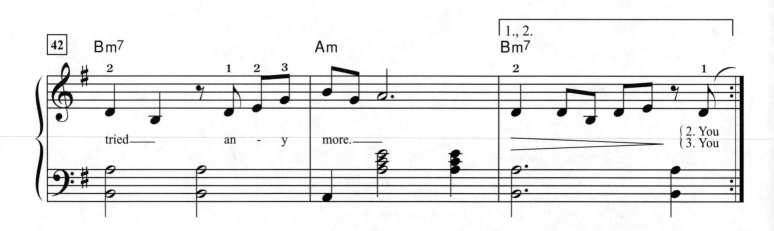

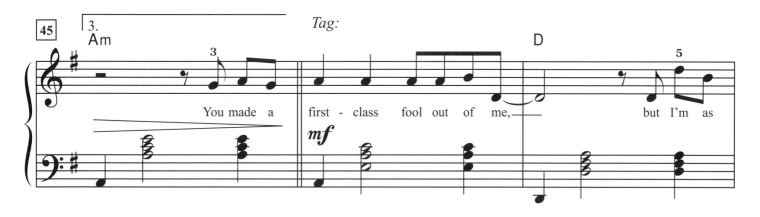

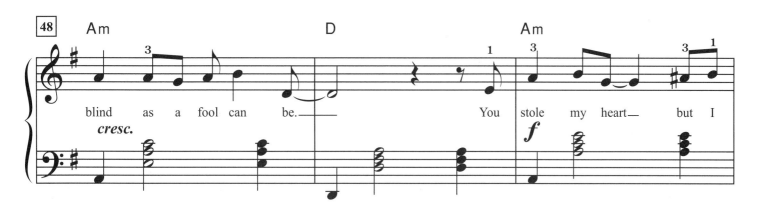

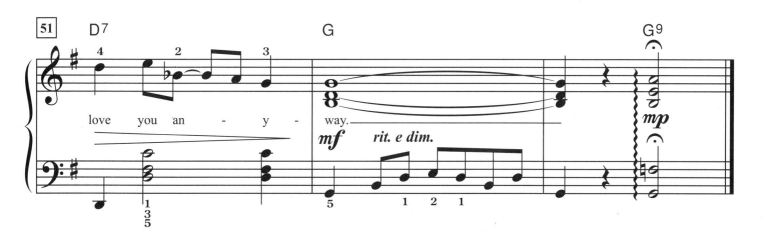

Verse 2:
You lured me away from home, just to save you from being alone.
You stole my soul, that's a pain I can do without.
All I needed was a friend to lend a guiding hand.
But you turned into a lover, and Mother, what a lover! You wore me out.
All you did was wreck my bed, and in the morning kick me in the head.
Oh, Maggie, I couldn't have tried anymore.

Verse 3:
You lured me away from home, 'cause you didn't want to be alone.
You stole my heart, I couldn't leave you if I tried.
I suppose I could collect my books and get back to school.
Or steal my Daddy's cue and make a living out of playin' pool,
Or find myself a rock and roll band that needs a helpin' hand.
Oh, Maggie, I wish I'd never seen your face.
(To Tag:)

THE MASTERPIECE
(Theme from "Masterpiece Theater")

Masterpiece Theatre premiered on PBS on January 10, 1971, introduced American audiences to quality British programming, and became America's longest-running primetime drama series. It has won 33 primetime Emmy Awards as well as 15 Peabody Awards. The theme music is the "Rondeau" from a baroque suite by French composer Jean-Joseph Mouret (1682–1738). It has become quite popular and is often used at wedding ceremonies.

By J.J. Mouret and Paul Parnes
Arranged by Dan Coates

MOONDANCE

Rock and Roll Hall of Fame inductee Van Morrison released his third solo album *Moondance* in 1970, and the title song was released as a single in 1977. The album's songs center around life in the country and are a mix of R & B, country rock, and jazz.

Words and Music by Van Morrison
Arranged by Dan Coates

skies.
And all the leaves on the trees are fall - ing to the
run.
And when you come, my heart will be wait - ing to make

sound of the breez-es that blow.
And I'm try - ing to please— to the call -
sure that you're nev - er a - lone.
There and then all my dreams— will come true,—

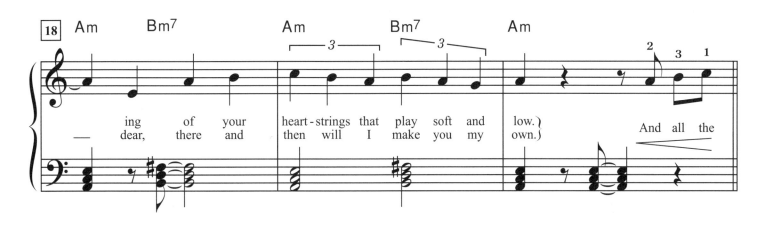

— ing of your heart-strings that play soft and low.)
dear, there and then will I make you my own.)
And all the

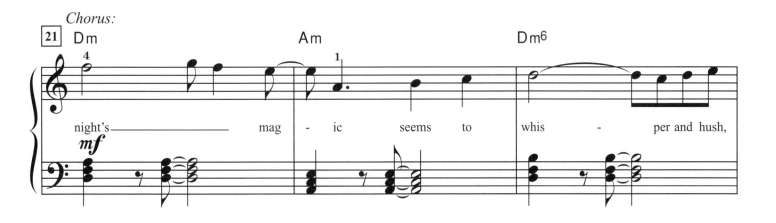

Chorus:

night's— mag - ic seems to whis - per and hush,

PEACEFUL EASY FEELING

The Eagles recorded "Peaceful Easy Feeling" in 1971–72 for their debut album *Eagles*. It was the third of three songs released from that album as singles, the other two being "Take It Easy" and "Witchy Woman." It was written in San Diego, California, and was influential in popularizing the southern California country rock sound in the early '70s.

Words and Music by Jack Tempchin
Arranged by Dan Coates

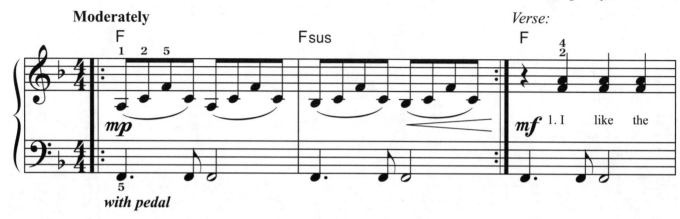

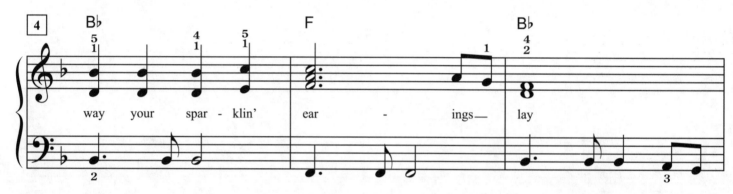

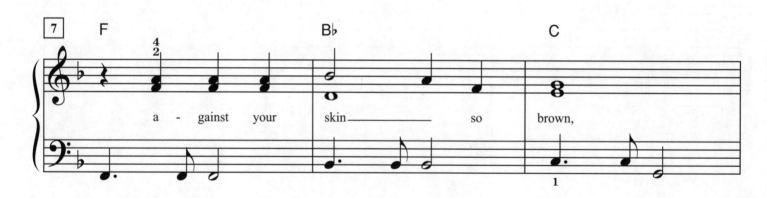

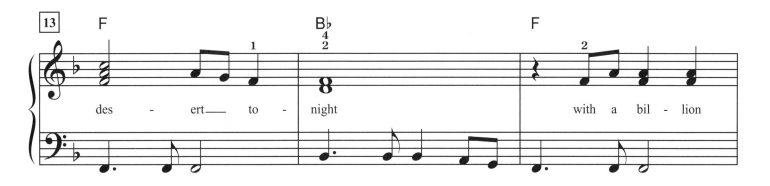

des - ert___ to - night   with a bil - lion

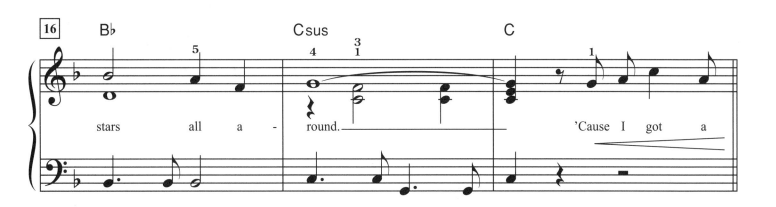

stars all a - round.___   'Cause I got a

Chorus:

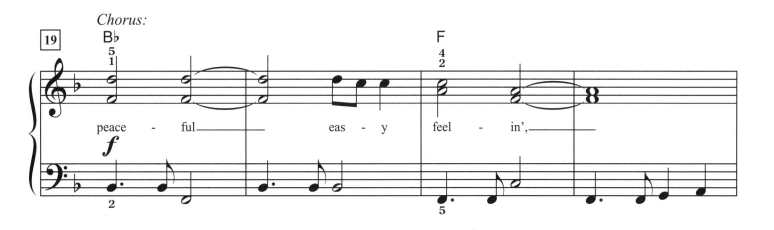

peace - ful___ eas - y feel - in',___

and I know you won't let me down,___

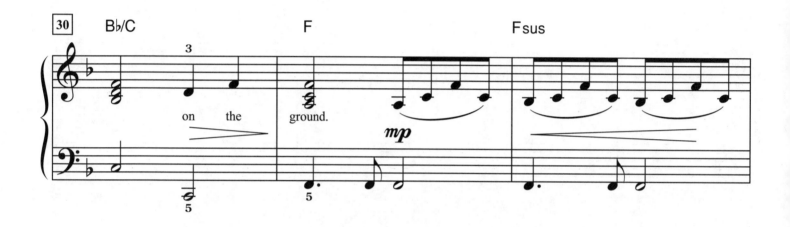

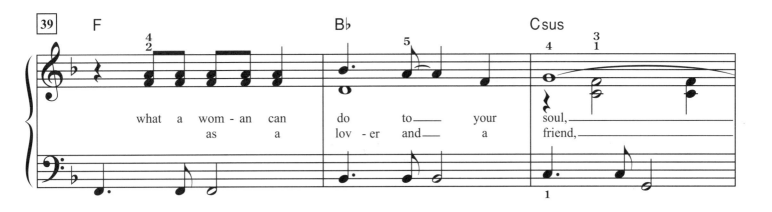

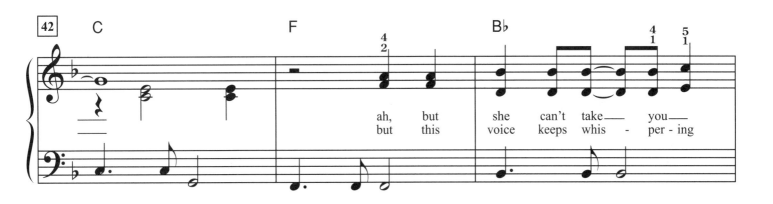

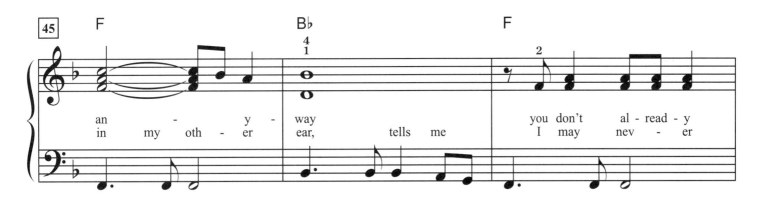

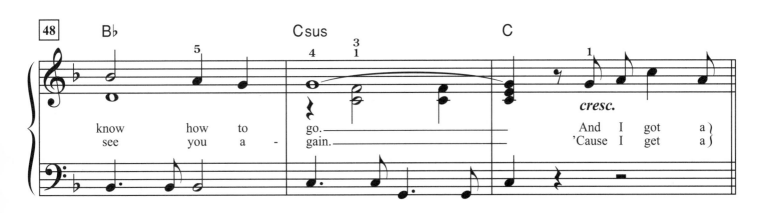

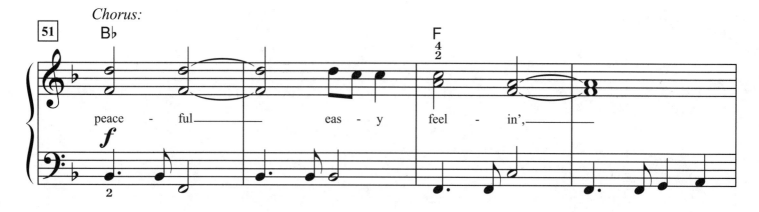

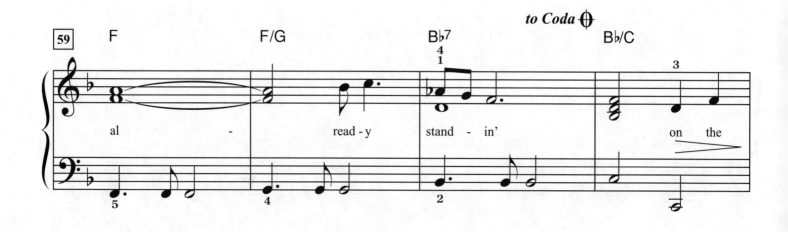

Coda

Bb/C F Gm7

I'm___ al - read - y

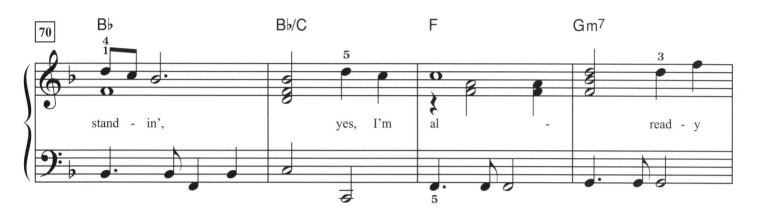

Bb Bb/C F Gm7

stand - in', yes, I'm al - read - y

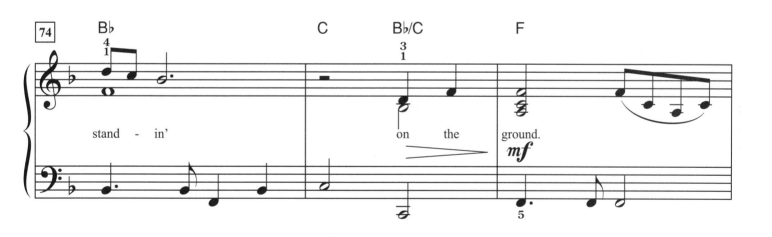

Bb C Bb/C F

stand - in' on the ground.

mf

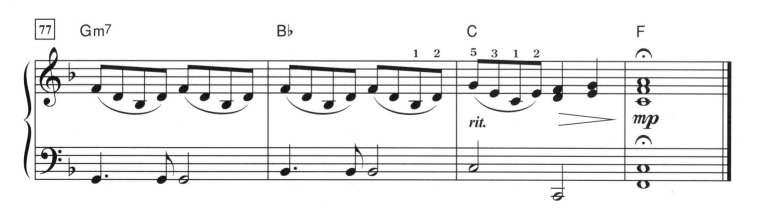

Gm7 Bb C F

rit. *mp*

SEND IN THE CLOWNS

Stephen Sondheim's *A Little Night Music* opened on Broadway at the Schubert Theatre in 1973. Based on the Ingmar Bergman film *Smiles of a Summer Night*, the story is a complex romance. "Send in the Clowns" is sung by the character Desiree Armfeldt, as a meditation on her unrequited love and on the state of her life.

Music and Lyrics by Stephen Sondheim
Arranged by Dan Coates

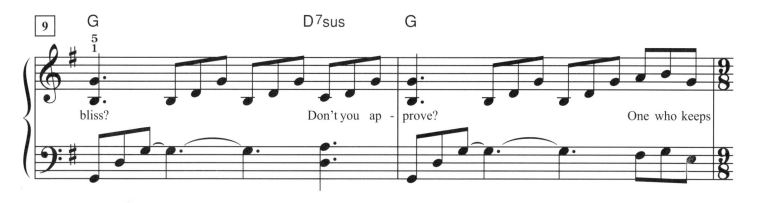

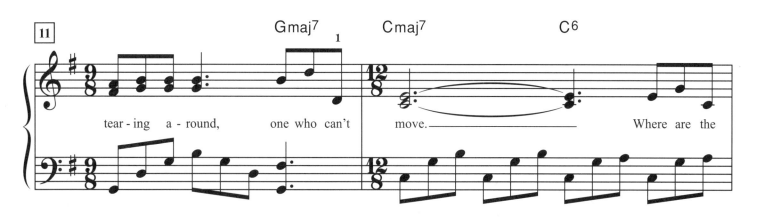

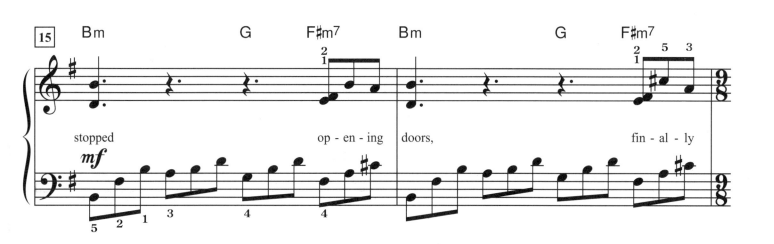

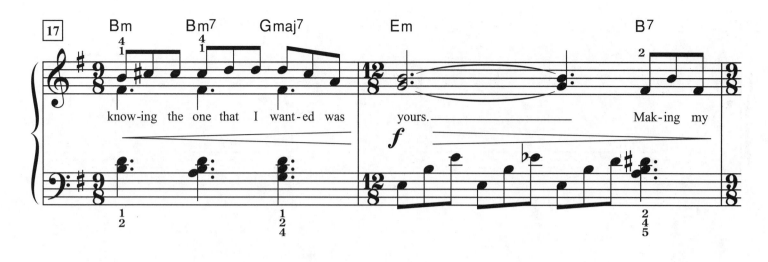

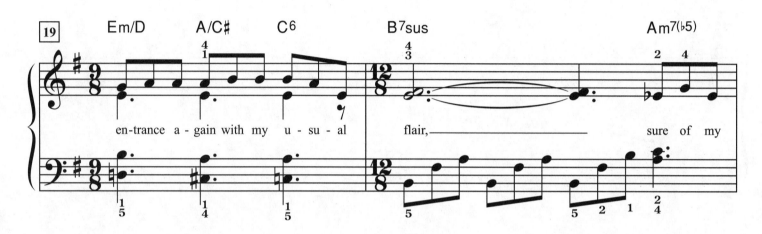

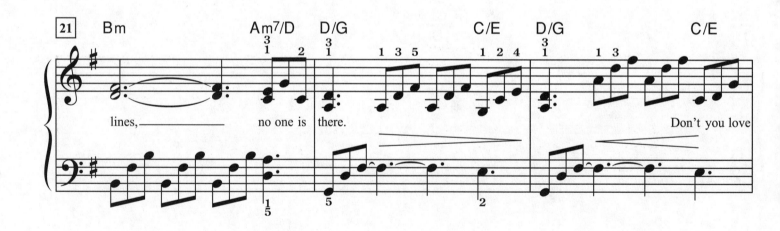

OLD TIME ROCK & ROLL

In 1978 Bob Seger & The Silver Bullet Band released *Stranger in Town*, their 10th album. "Old Time Rock and Roll" was the third track on the album and became tremendously popular. In 1983 it was featured in the movie *Risky Business* in a famous dance scene starring Tom Cruise. In 2001 the Recording Industry Association of America chose it as one of the Songs of the Century.

Words and Music by
George Jackson and Thomas E. Jones III
Arranged by Dan Coates

Bright rock beat

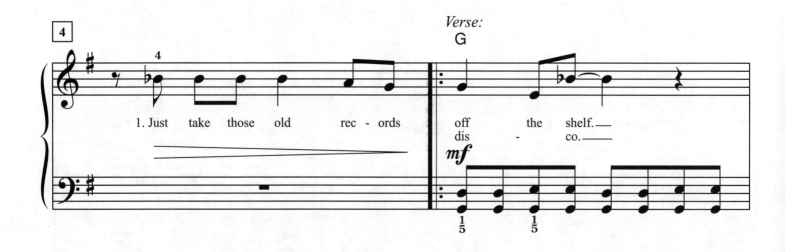

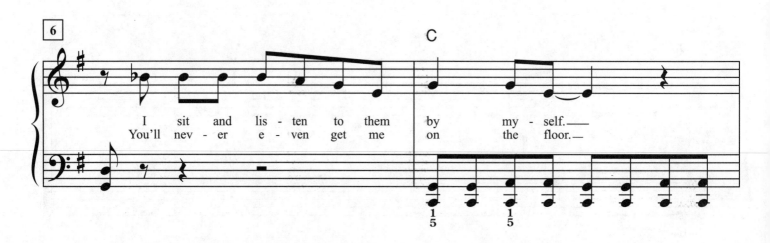

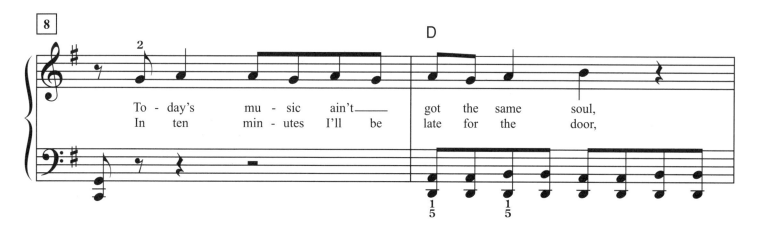

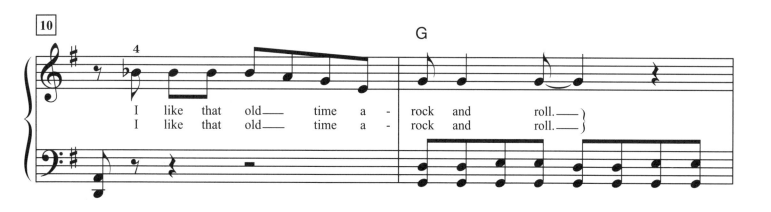

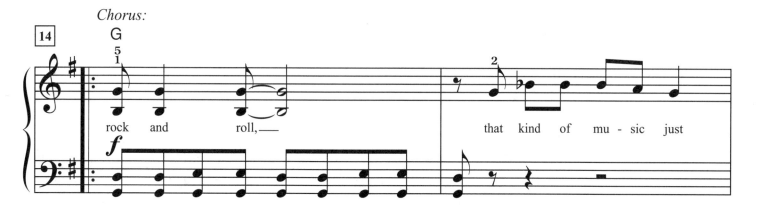

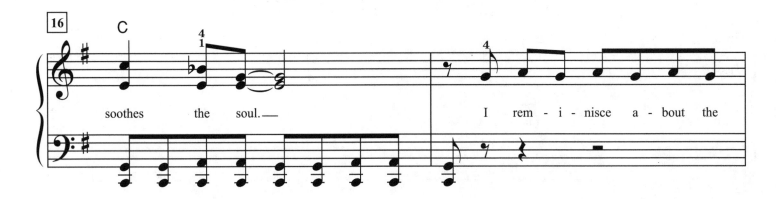

soothes the soul.— I rem - i - nisce a - bout the

days of old— with that old—— time a -

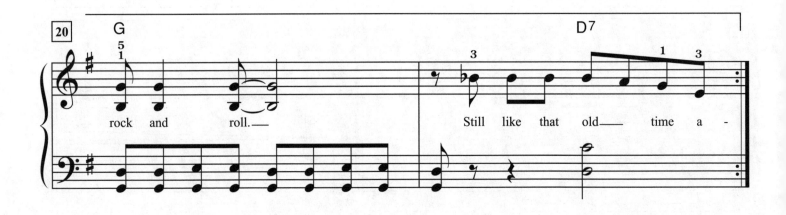

rock and roll.— Still like that old— time a -

with that— old— time a - rock and roll.—

SISTER GOLDEN HAIR

The English-American band America recorded their fifth album, *Hearts,* in 1975 in Sausalito, California, with the help of Beatles producer George Martin. "Sister Golden Hair" is the most famous song from that album and reach the top of the Billboard Hot 100.

Words and Music by Gerry Beckley
Arranged by Dan Coates

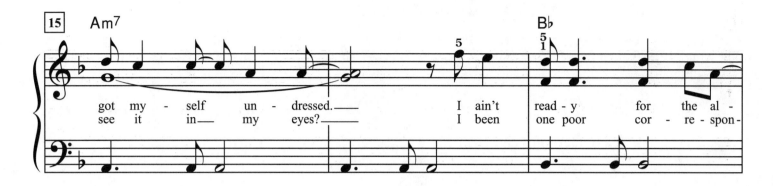

dle, will you— meet me in the air?— Will you love me just a lit -

tle, just e - nough to show you care?— Though I tried to fake— it,

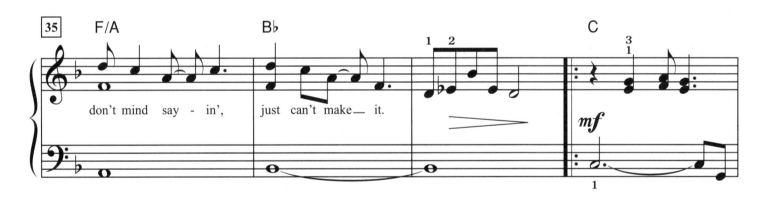

don't mind say - in', just can't make— it.

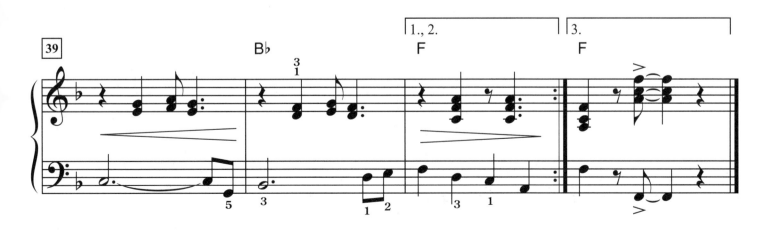

SONG FROM M*A*S*H
(Suicide Is Painless)

*M*A*S*H* is a 1970 comedic film by director Robert Altman about medical personnel at a Mobile Army Surgical Hospital (MASH). The film was based on a novel by Richard Hooker, *MASH: A Novel About Three Army Doctors,* set against the backdrop of the Korean War. The film was turned into a television series of the same name which ran on CBS from 1972 to 1983 and garnered a total of 14 Emmy Awards. The series finale was the most-watched television broadcast in history. The theme music was written by Johnny Mandel with lyrics written by Altman's 14-year-old son, Mike Altman.

Words and Music by
Mike Altman and Johnny Mandel
Arranged by Dan Coates

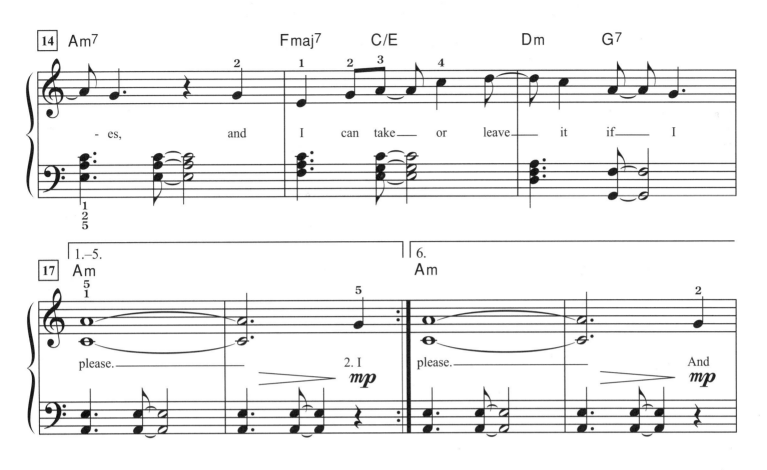

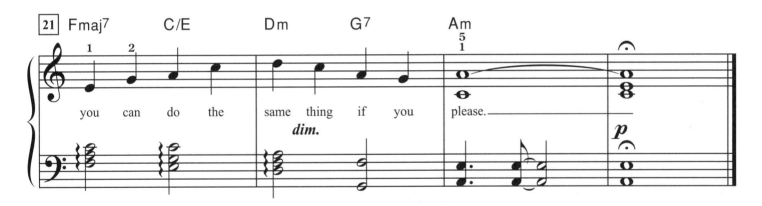

Verse 2:
I try to find a way to make
All our little joys relate
Without that ever-present hate
But now I know that it's too late.
And *(To Chorus:)*

Verse 3:
The game of life is hard to play,
I'm going to lose it anyway,
The losing card I'll someday lay,
So that is all I have to say,
That *(To Chorus:)*

Verse 4:
The only way you win is cheat,
And lay it down before I'm beat,
And to another give a seat,
For that's the only painless feat.
'Cause *(To Chorus:)*

Verse 5:
The sword of time will pierce our skins,
It doesn't hurt when it begins,
But as it works its way on in
The pain grows stronger, watch it grin.
For *(To Chorus:)*

Verse 6:
A brave man once requested me
To answer questions that are key,
Is it to be or not to be?
And I replied, "Oh, why ask me?"
'Cause *(To Chorus:)*

STAR WARS (MAIN TITLE)

On May 25, 1977 George Lucas introduced the world to *Star Wars,* one of the most successful, popular and influential films of all time, a science fiction masterpiece. The movie's dazzling special effects not only won over an ongoing fan base but also directed the film industry's focus to big-budget blockbuster productions. The film's soundtrack—performed by the London Symphony Orchestra with John Williams conducting—was voted #1 by the American Film Institute in 2005.

By **JOHN WILLIAMS**
Arranged by Dan Coates

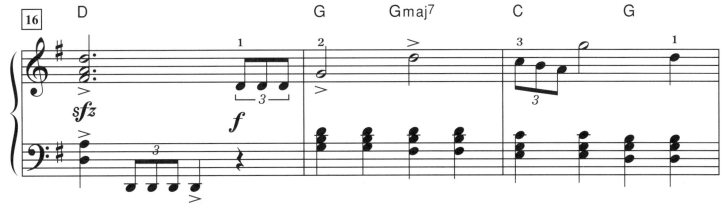

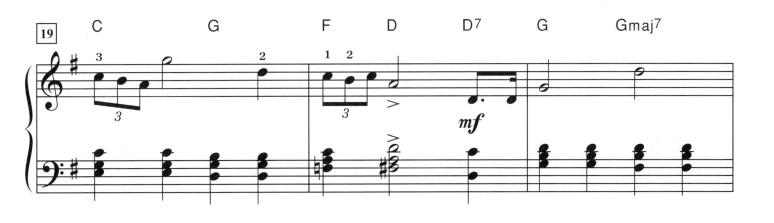

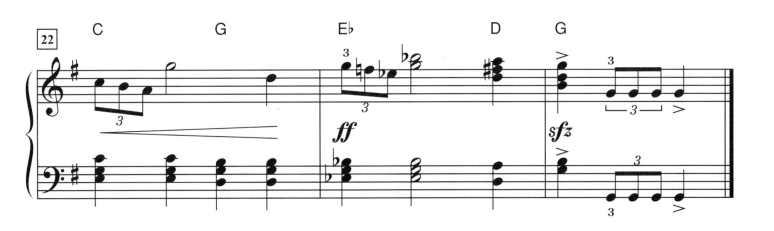

STAYIN' ALIVE

Disco originated in the United States in the early '70s, derived from funk and soul music, and the term "disco" originated from the French word "discothèque" meaning nightclub. A number of musicians were well known for this up-tempo dance music: ABBA, Barry White, Diana Ross, Donna Summer, Gloria Gaynor, The Jackson 5, KC and The Sunshine Band, and the Village People, to name a few. The 1977 film *Saturday Night Fever* helped established disco as a genre. The Bee Gees' "Stayin' Alive" was the first track on the soundtrack for the film and provided the music for the opening scene.

Words and Music by Barry Gibb,
Maurice Gibb and Robin Gibb
Arranged by Dan Coates

THE SUMMER KNOWS
(Theme from "Summer of '42")

Summer of '42 is a 1971 coming-of-age film about a boy who falls in love with a married woman while on summer vacation on Nantucket island. It is based on the memoirs of screenwriter Herman Raucher. Michel Legrand's romantic theme music has a poignant moment when the two main characters in the film slowly dance to it.

Words by Marilyn and Alan Bergman
Music by Michel Legrand
Arranged by Dan Coates

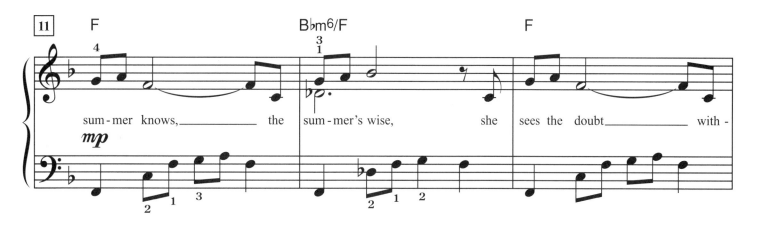

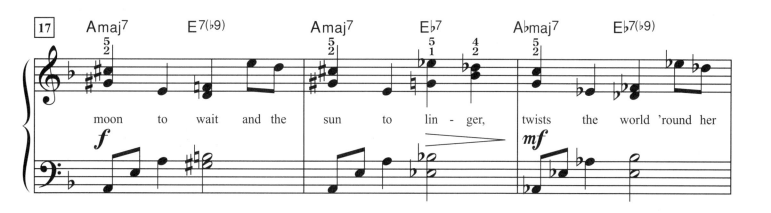

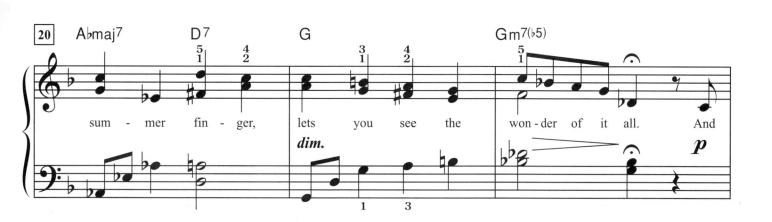

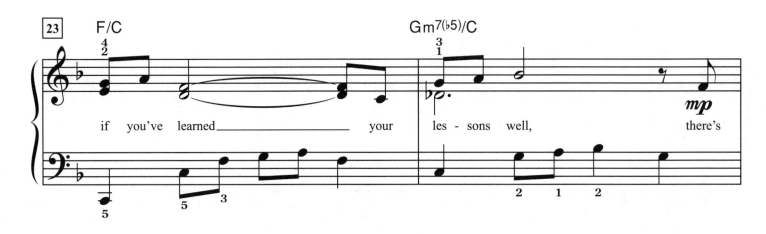

if you've learned _____ your les - sons well, there's

lit - tle more _____ for her to tell. One

last ca - ress, it's time to dress for fall. _____

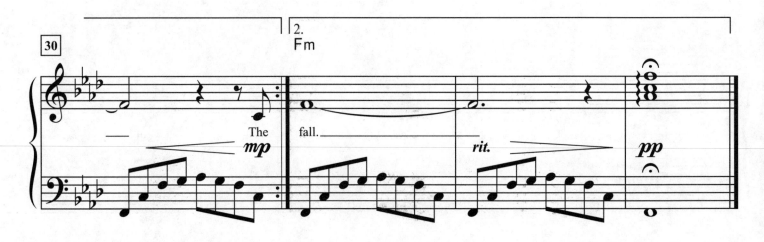

The fall. _____

SUNSHINE ON MY SHOULDERS

John Denver's "Sunshine on My Shoulders" was released in 1973 and peaked at #1 on the charts. Denver mentioned that the song was written with only thoughts of spring in mind, but the song gained significance as the Vietnam War ended and Americans used it as a beacon of hope for the future.

Words by John Denver
Music by John Denver, Mike Taylor and Dick Kniss
Arranged by Dan Coates

THEME FROM "SUPERMAN"

Released in 1978, *Superman* was the first blockbuster film adaptation of a comic book superhero. The original character of Superman was created by American writer Jerry Siegel and Canadian-born artist Joe Shuster in 1932 and first appeared in *Action Comics #1* (June, 1938), helping to establish the superhero genre and the American comic book. Superman found popularity on the radio, on television, and even on Broadway, but found new life and a new audience in the 1978 film.

By **JOHN WILLIAMS**
Arranged by Dan Coates

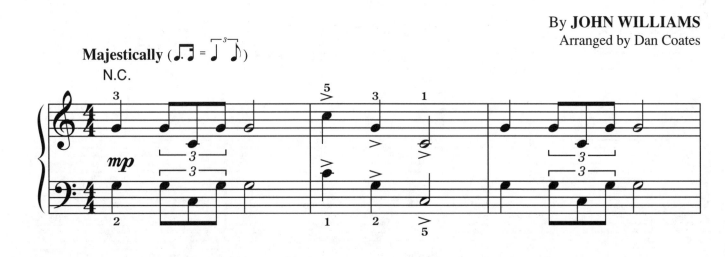

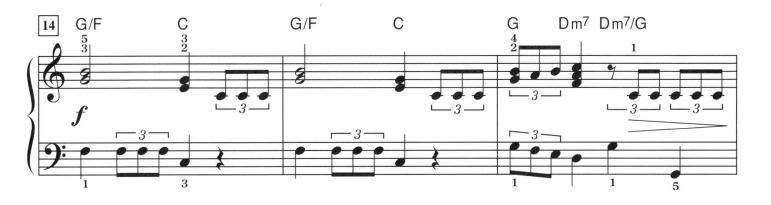

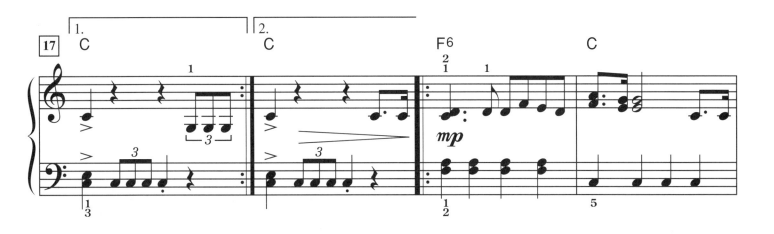

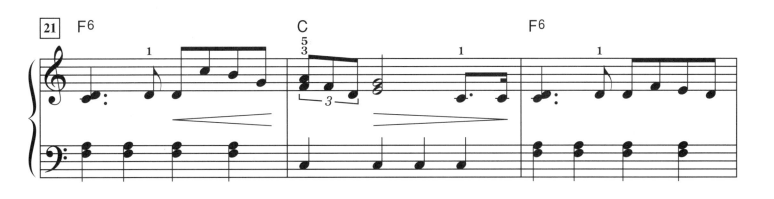

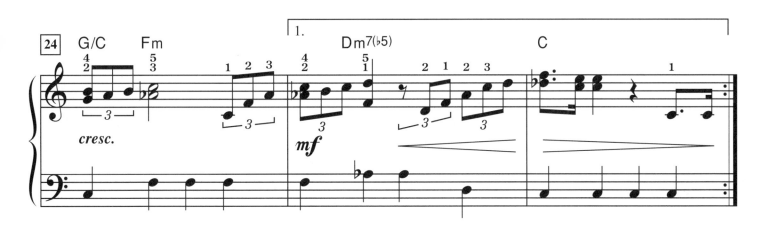

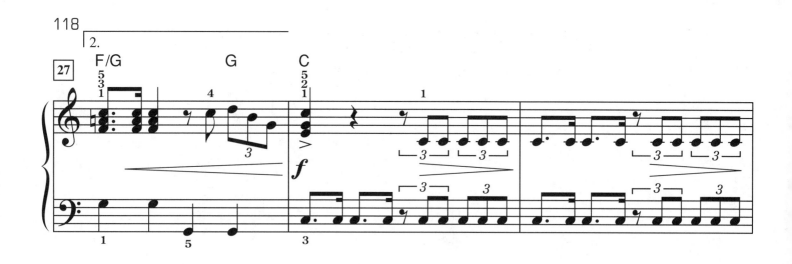

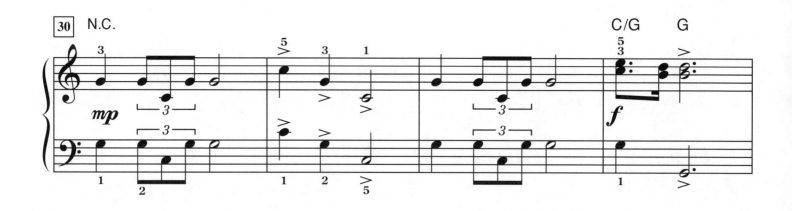

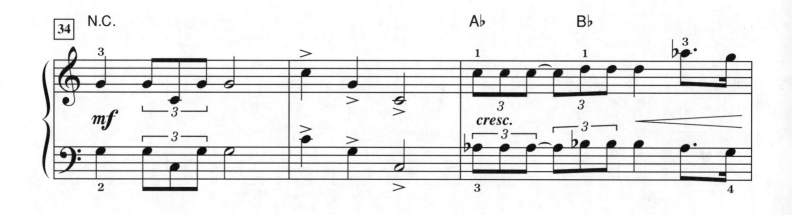

THOSE WERE THE DAYS
(from "All in the Family")

All in the Family was originally broadcast on the CBS television network from January 12, 1971 to April 8, 1979. It starred Carroll O'Connor as Archie Bunker, a working-class, outspoken bigot, and his family who lived in Queens, New York. The sit-com ranked #1 in the yearly Nielsen ratings from 1972 to 1976, and *TV Guide* named Archie Bunker television's greatest character of all time. Archie and his wife Edith (Jean Stapleton) sing the nostalgic "Those Were the Days" at their spinet piano at the start of every episode in front of a live audience, which foreshadows the political nature of the show to follow.

Music by Charles Strouse
Words by Lee Adams
Arranged by Dan Coates

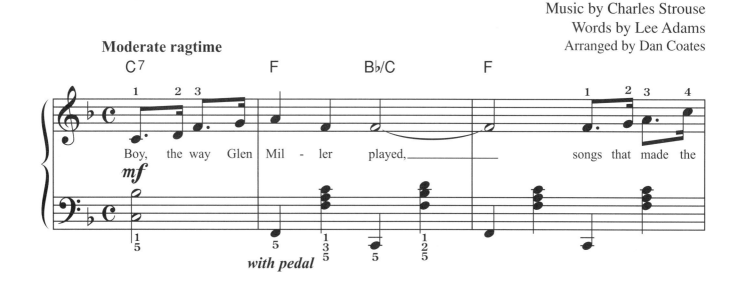

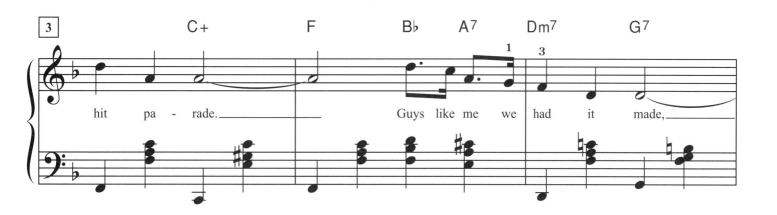

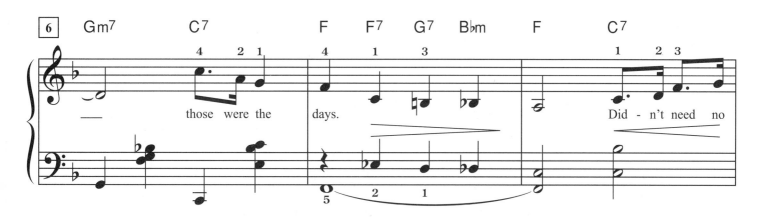

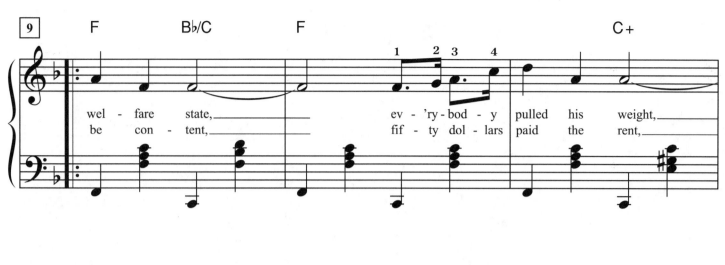

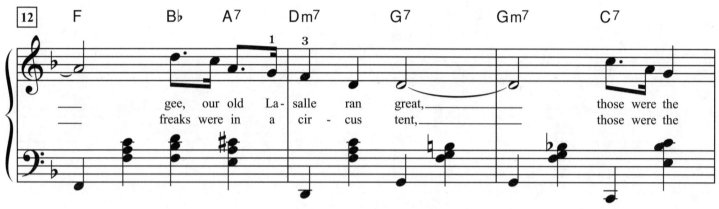

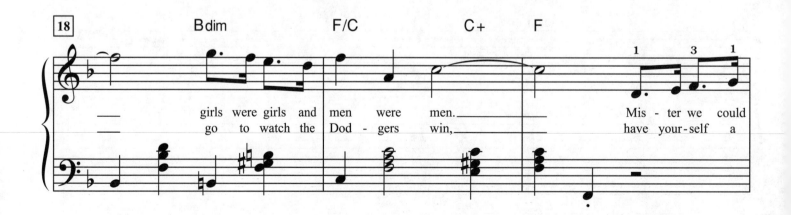

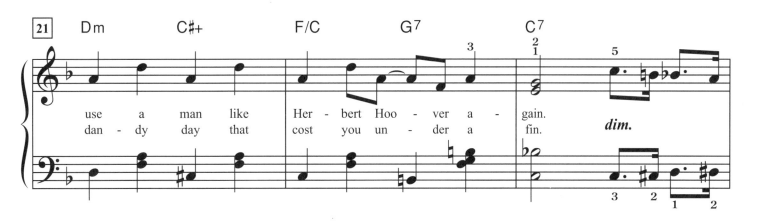

use a man like Her - bert Hoo - ver a - gain.
dan - dy day that cost you un - der a fin.

dim.

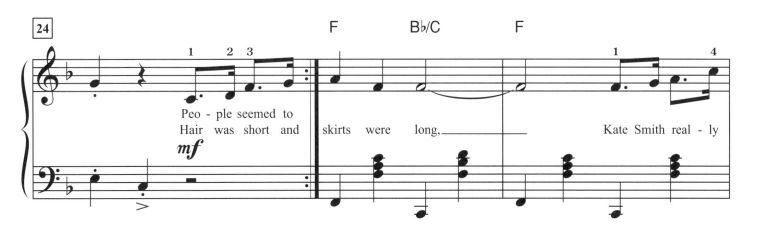

Peo - ple seemed to
Hair was short and skirts were long,_____ Kate Smith real - ly

mf

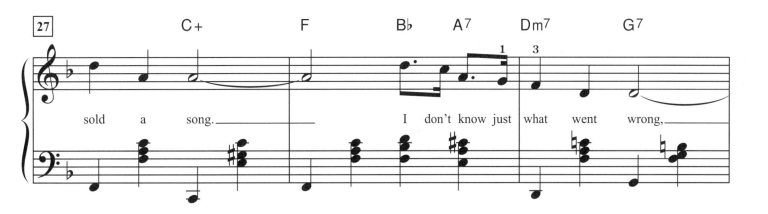

sold a song._____ I don't know just what went wrong,_____

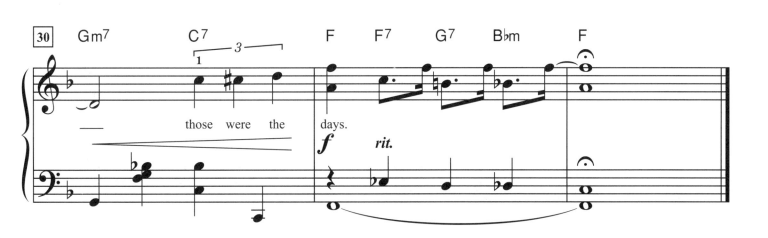

_____ those were the days.

f *rit.*

WEEKEND IN NEW ENGLAND

Barry Manilow released "Weekend in New England" on his fourth studio album *This One's for You* (1976). The album went triple-platinum and also contained the hits "Daybreak" and "Looks Like We Made It." The '70s was a very fruitful decade for Manilow; he worked with many industry legends including Bette Midler, Clive Davis, Penny Marshall, Ray Charles, John Denver, and Dionne Warwick. The '70s also saw the debuts of his hits "Mandy" and "Copacabana."

Words and Music by Randy Edelman
Arranged by Dan Coates

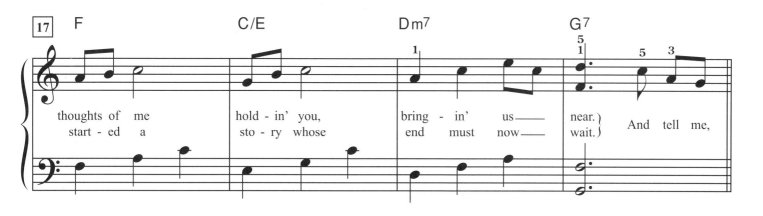

17 F / C/E / Dm7 / G7

thoughts of me / hold - in' you, / bring - in' us—— near.
start - ed a / sto - ry whose / end must now—— wait.
And tell me,

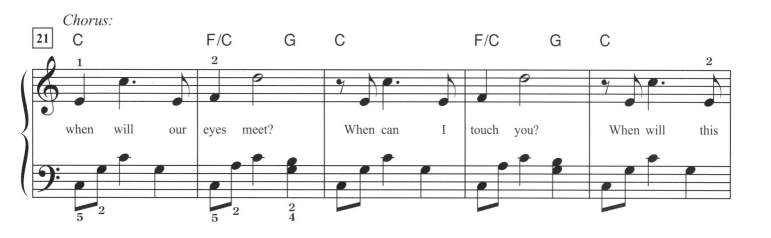

Chorus:

21 C / F/C G C / F/C G C

when will our eyes meet? / When can I touch you? / When will this

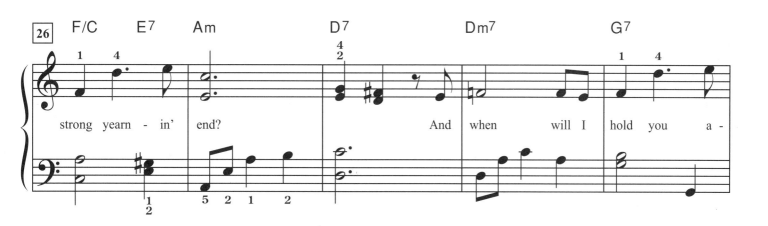

26 F/C E7 Am / D7 / Dm7 / G7

strong yearn - in' end? / And when will I hold you a-

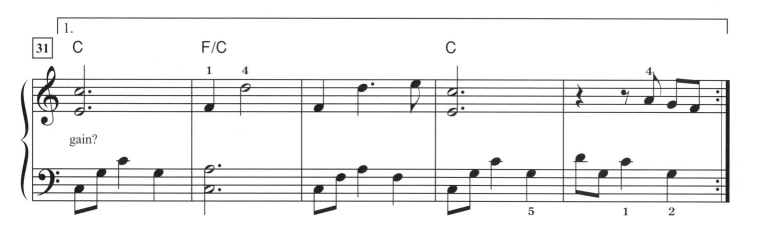

1.

31 C / F/C / C

gain?

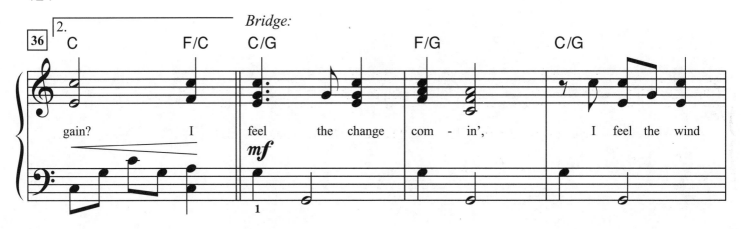

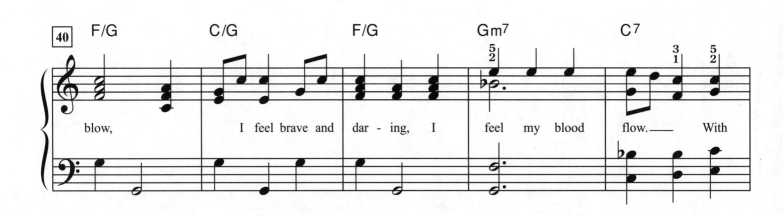

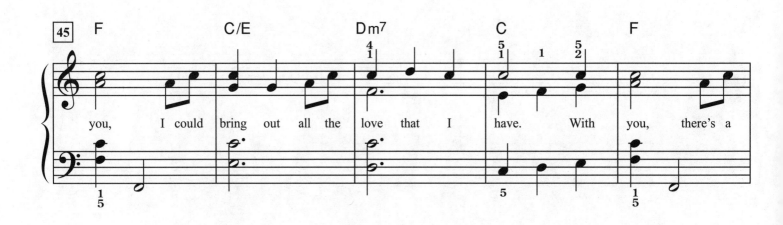

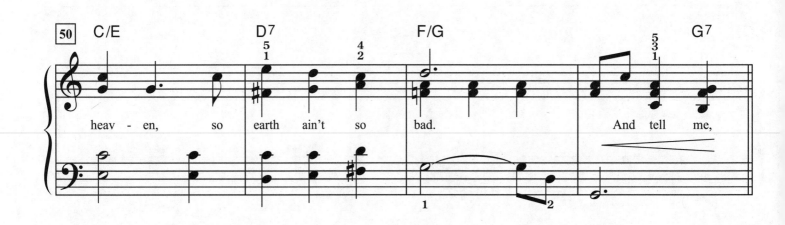

Chorus:

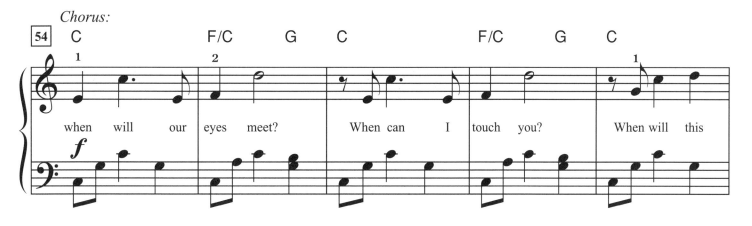

when will our eyes meet? When can I touch you? When will this

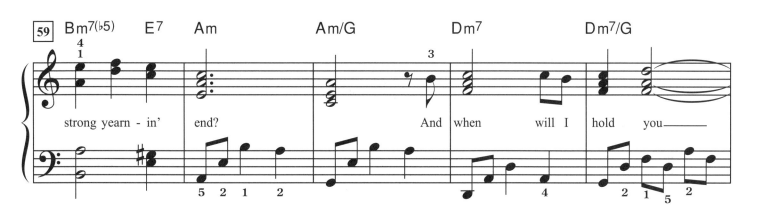

strong yearn - in' end? And when will I hold you

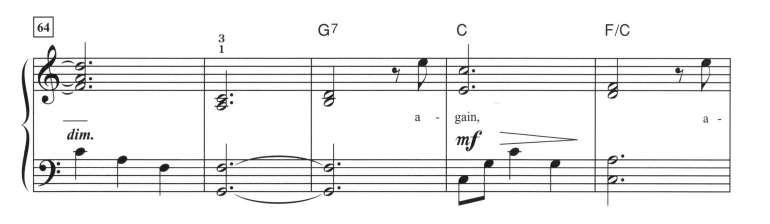

a - gain, a -

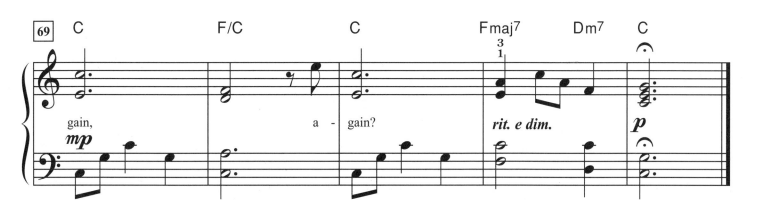

gain, a - gain?

WHAT A FOOL BELIEVES

The Doobie Brothers recorded "What a Fool Believes" for their 1978 album *Minute by Minute*. The single reached #1 on the Billboard Hot 100 in 1979, and the album would earn triple platinum status. Both the song and the album won Grammy Awards in 1980.

Words and Music by
Michael McDonald and Kenny Loggins
Arranged by Dan Coates

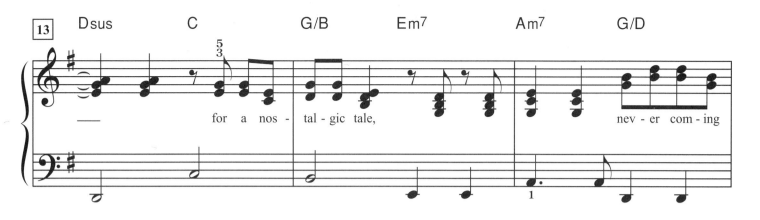

for a nos - tal - gic tale,　　never com - ing

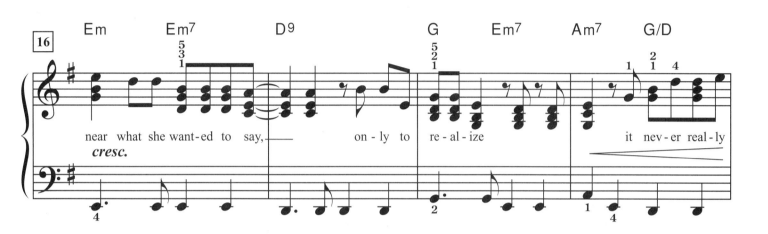

near what she want-ed to say,　only to re - al - ize　it nev-er real - ly

cresc.

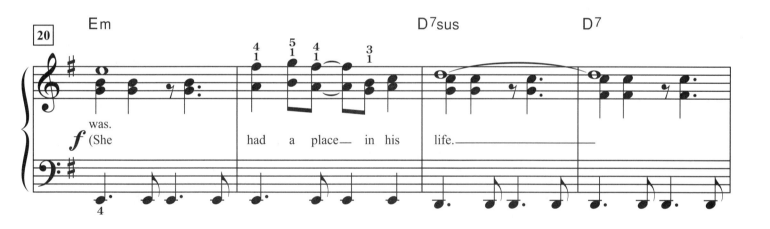

was. (She　had a place　in his　life.

f

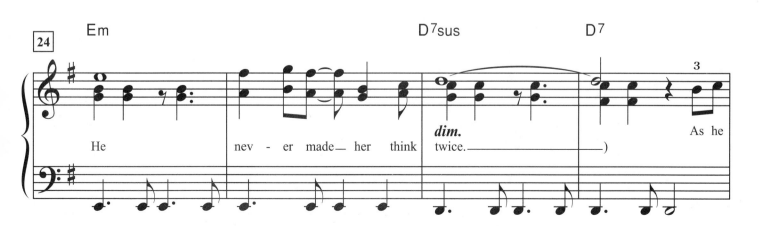

He　nev - er made　her think twice.　　As he

dim.

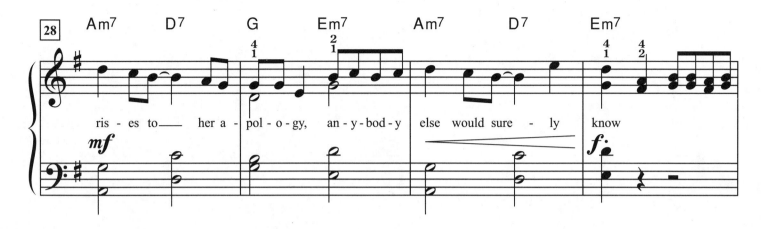

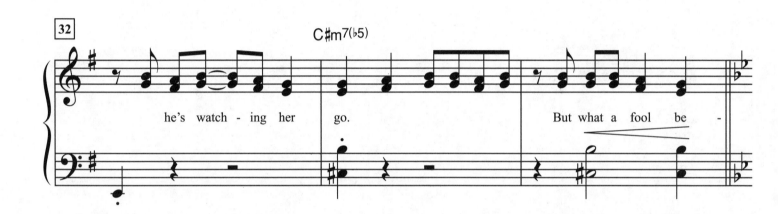

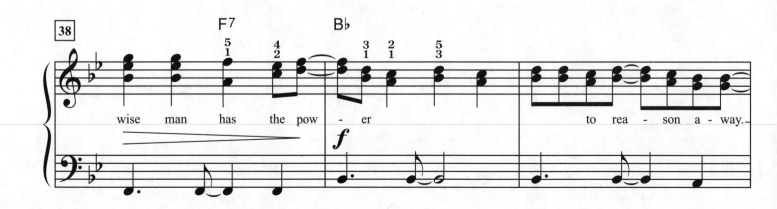

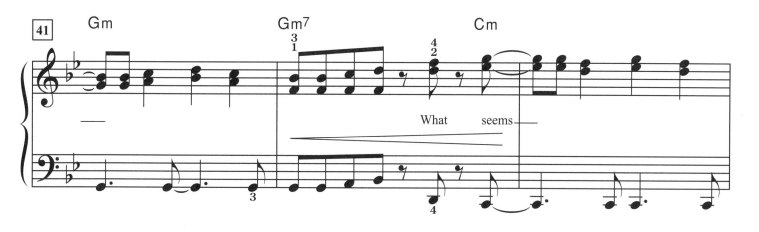

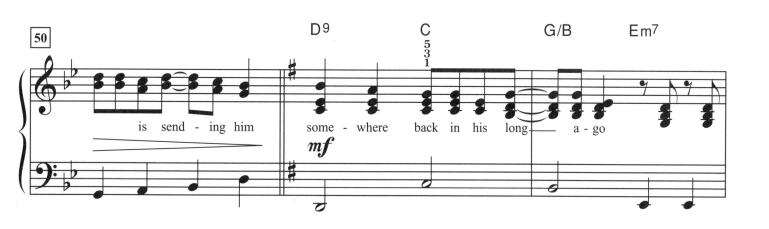

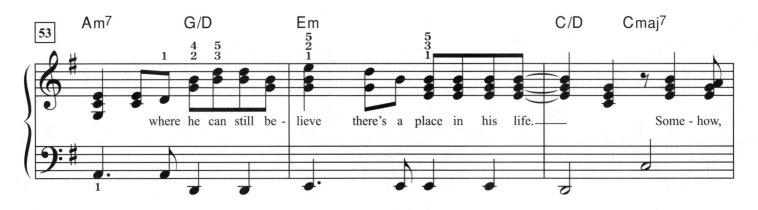

where he can still be - lieve there's a place in his life. Some - how,

some - day, she will re - turn!

cresc.

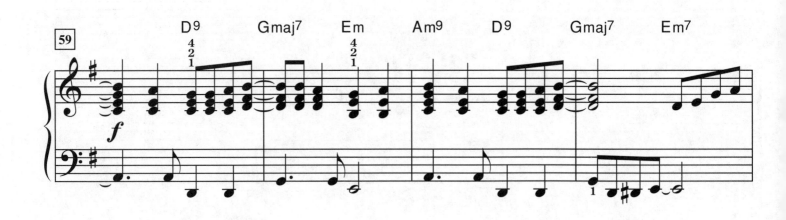

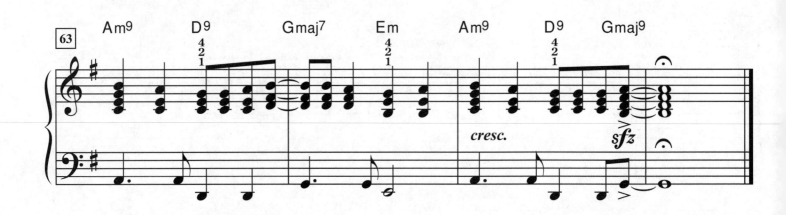

TOO YOUNG

Nat King Cole recorded "Too Young" in 1951. The record sold over a million copies and stayed at #1 on the Billboard charts for five weeks. In 1972 Donny Osmond recorded it as a single which peaked at #13. Osmond was one of the most popular teen idols in the early '70s, and later in the decade he would team up with his little sister, Marie, to record several albums and host a television variety show.

Words by Sylvia Dee
Music by Sid Lippman
Arranged by Dan Coates

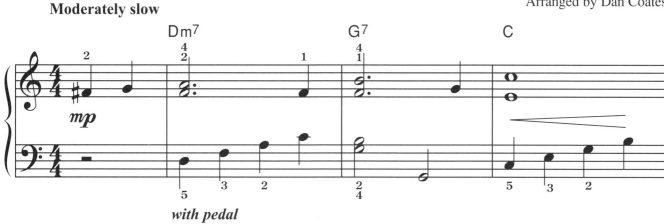

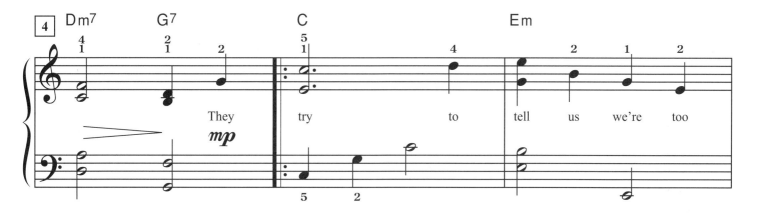

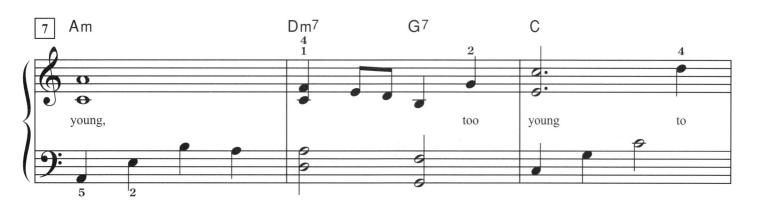

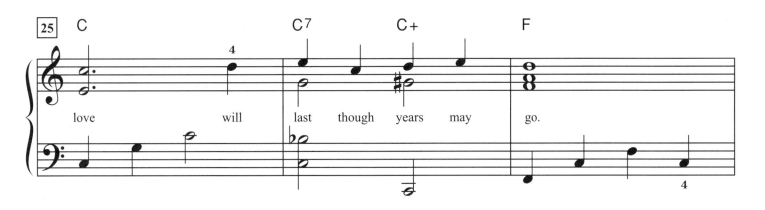

25 C   C7   C+   F

love   will   last   though   years   may   go.

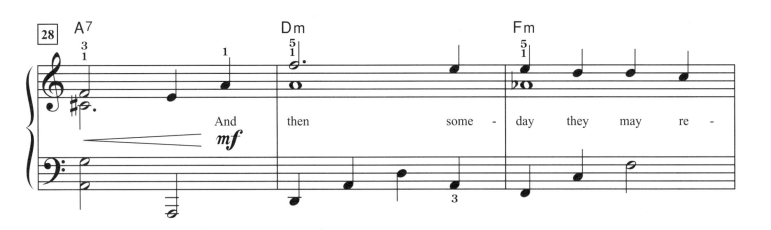

28 A7   Dm   Fm

mf   And   then   some - day   they   may   re -

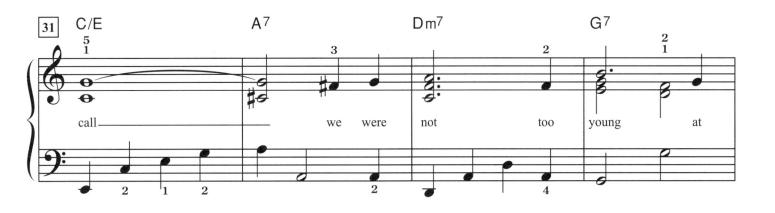

31 C/E   A7   Dm7   G7

call_____   we   were   not   too   young   at

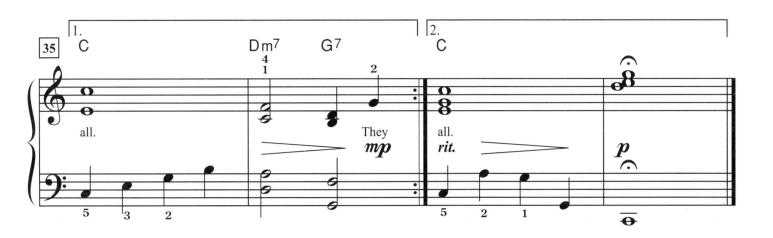

1. 35 C   Dm7   G7   2. C

all.   They   all.   *mp*   *rit.*   *p*

YOU MAKE ME FEEL BRAND NEW

"You Make Me Feel Brand New" was recorded by the Philadelphia soul group The Stylistics in 1974. It became their biggest U.S. hit, peaking at #2 on the charts. The song has been covered by Boyz II Men, Roberta Flack, and Simply Red.

Words and Music by
Thom Bell and Linda Creed
Arranged by Dan Coates

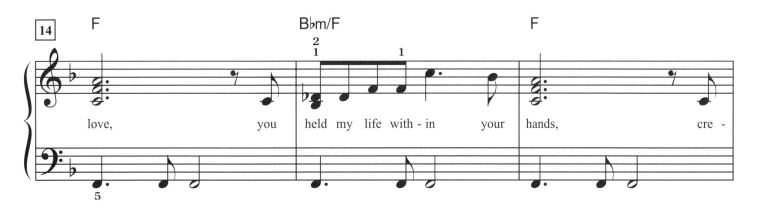

love, you held my life with-in your hands, cre -

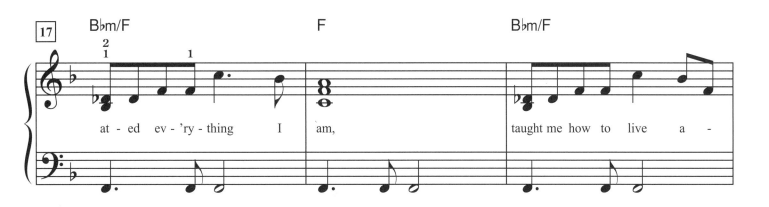

at - ed ev - 'ry - thing I am, taught me how to live a -

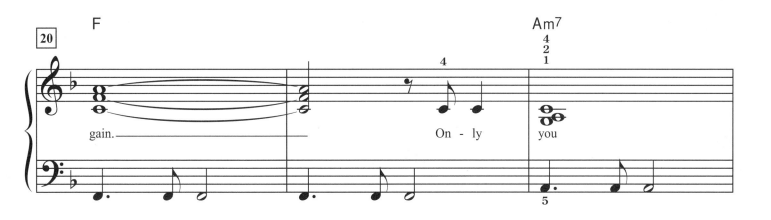

gain. On - ly you

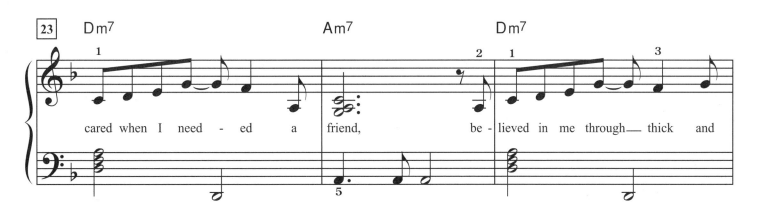

cared when I need - ed a friend, be - lieved in me through thick and

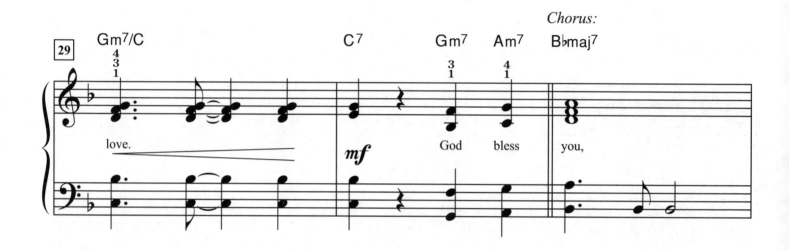

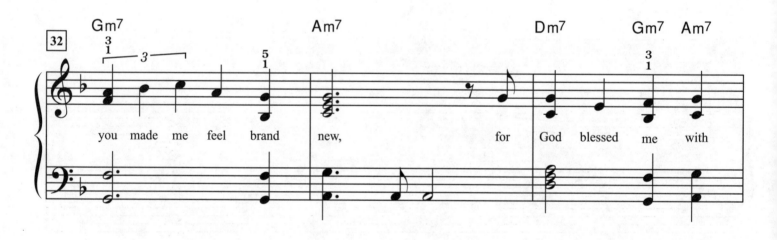

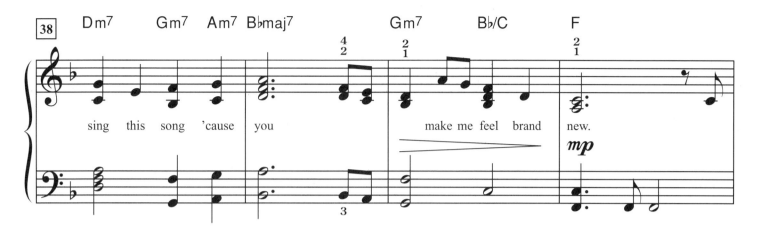

sing this song 'cause you make me feel brand new.

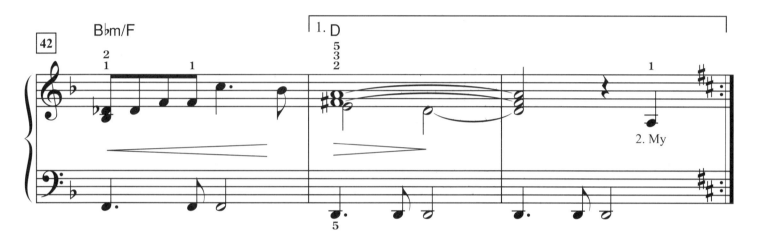

Verse 2:
My love,
Whenever I was insecure,
You built me up and made me sure.
You gave my pride back to me.
Precious friend,
With you I'll always have a friend.
You're someone who I can depend
To walk a path that sometimes bends.
Without you,
Life has no meaning or rhyme,
Like notes to a song out of time.
How can I repay you for having faith in me?
(To Chorus:)

YOU LIGHT UP MY LIFE

"You Light Up My Life" was written for the 1977 romantic comedy/drama of the same name. Kasey Cisyk recorded the song for the movie, and Debby Boone, who is the daughter of '50s icon Pat Boone, recorded and released the song as a single. The single topped the Billboard Hot 100 for 10 weeks and became the most successful single of the '70s.

Words and Music by Joe Brooks
Arranged by Dan Coates

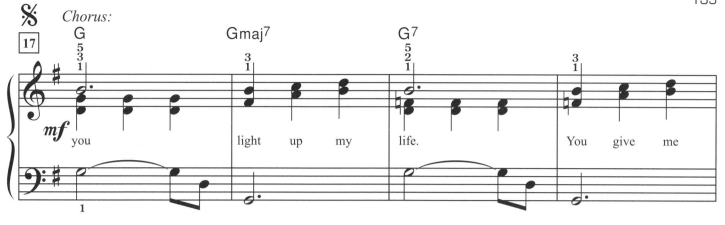

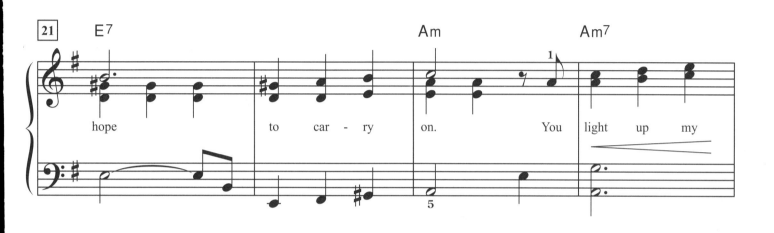

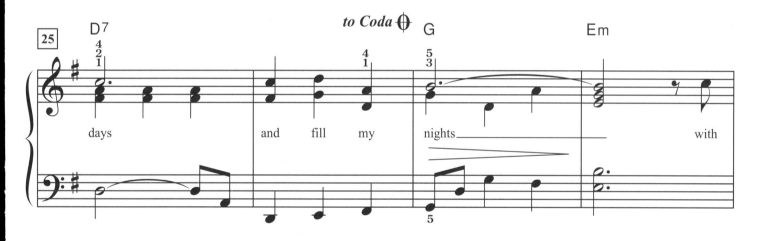

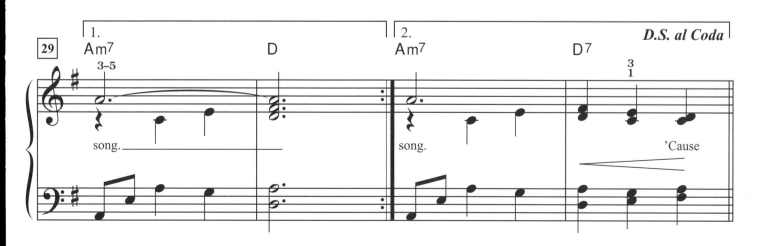

YOU NEEDED ME

"You Needed Me" was a #1 single for Canadian singer Anne Murray in 1978. Murray is often cited as the woman who paved the way for other Canadian international success stories: Celine Dion, Sarah McLachlan, and Shania Twain. The song was also covered by the Irish boy band Boyzone in 1999 and was #1 on the U.K. charts.

Words and Music by Randy Goodrum
Arranged by Dan Coates